When Christians Gather

Issues in the Celebration of Eucharist

PAULIST PRESS
New York / Mahwah, N.J.

Cover design by John Petersen

The Publisher acknowledges Compass: A Review of Topical Theology (30 [1996]: 8–15) for some sections of chapter 5 that first appeared there in an article by the author entitled "Negotiating the Sunday Eucharist: Communication, Negotiation and Distortion."

Library of Congress Cataloging-in-Publication Data

Darragh, Neil, 1942–
    When Christians gather : issues in the celebration of Eucharist / Neil Darragh.
        p. cm.
    Includes bibliographical references.
    ISBN 0-8091-3678-3 (alk. paper)
    1. Lord's Supper—Catholic Church. 2. Catholic Church—Liturgy. I. Title.
BX2215.2.D37   1996
264'.02036—dc20   96-32676
                                                                        CIP

Published by Paulist Press
997 Macarthur Boulevard
Mahwah, New Jersey 07430

Printed and bound in the United States of America

Contents

Introduction

From time to time, in the midst of liturgical celebration or liturgical discussion or liturgical despair, we wonder whether we have overlooked the central issues.

Only a few of the numerous points that are discussed by liturgy committees and congregations, ministers, priests, and liturgists are central to the life of the Christian community. The peripheries of the Eucharist seem somehow to attract more attention than the central issues. Perhaps these latter are simply too difficult to deal with. Perhaps they just take too much time. The pressure of what has to be done tomorrow, what has to be organized immediately, or what we are going to do this coming Sunday may be too strong to leave time or energy for the larger issues with no clear solutions. And in any case, the central issues are too disturbing or too sensitive to be faced with any tranquillity or pleasure. This book is an attempt to name and discuss some central issues in what we do at Eucharist.

The central issues are not the most generalized. They are not to do with how things used to be, nor with a golden age of liturgy in the past. Nor are they, at least initially, to do with the deep symbolic meaning of bread and wine, or priesthood, or the nature of God's word. For the most part and most importantly they are about what we actually do at Eucharist. It is what we actually do during a Eucharist that constitutes the symbolism of Eucharist.

Bread and wine are just abstractions until people actually take a piece of bread and a container of wine, and hold them, or offer them, or talk about them, or declare things about them, or pray over them, or give them to others, or receive them from others, or

1

eat and drink them. Similarly, God's word is just an abstraction or a beautiful metaphor until *someone*, not just anyone but someone with a particular face and voice and personality, *proclaims words*, not just any words but very particular selected words in a particular language with a particular accent and intonation. And these words are proclaimed to a particular *audience*, not just any audience but particular people with particular shapes and clothing and colors and postures. All these particularities go to make up the symbolism of the Eucharists we *actually* celebrate as distinct from the ones we talk about or write about.

We deal best with these issues when they are very precisely focused. Liturgical symbols are very concrete acts of communication. The effects of such communication may differ from community to community, from culture to culture, and from nation to nation. A critical reflection on the symbolism of Christian gathering in Eucharist cannot assume that all Eucharists are the same everywhere. Such reflection has to begin with particular communities conscious of their own particular social and cultural circumstances. What appear as central issues in one community may not be so in another. This does not mean that our reflections have to be completely confined to within our own communities without possibility of enrichment or critique *between* communities and cultures. Problems or issues discovered and analyzed in one community invite other communities to consider whether these are also their issues. Solutions attempted in one community suggest solutions for other communities.

The reflections which I offer in this book are drawn from that part of the Christian community which I know best, and in which the central issues appear to me most clearly. Thus these reflections draw upon that Christian liturgical tradition with which I am most familiar, namely, the Roman Catholic tradition, within the cultural context with which I am most familiar, namely, that of New Zealanders of European descent.

Aotearoa New Zealand is a group of islands in the South Pacific Ocean. It has been inhabited by the indigenous Maori people for something over a thousand years. European migration began in some numbers in the early nineteenth century, and by the late nineteenth century the European settlers outnumbered the Maori. The total current population of the nation is just on three and a half million. The indigenous Maori constitute 10% of the population. People of European descent are just under 80%. Those whose ethnic origins are in Pacific islands to the north of Aotearoa New Zealand (Samoa, Cook Islands, Tonga, Tokelau, Niue, Fiji) constitute about 4%. Those of Chinese or Indian origin constitute about 1% each.

These ethnic identifications are important liturgically since each grouping retains its own languages and ritual styles. Each ethnic group, therefore, has its own agenda for liturgical inculturation. This book is concerned entirely with the agenda of New Zealanders of European descent, commonly known as "Pakeha," which is the ethnic group to which I belong. This agenda is influenced by the other active liturgical agendas within Aotearoa New Zealand, mainly Maori, Samoan, and Tongan. But the sensitivities of multicultural and bicultural relationships require that each ethnic group be in charge of its own agenda. The agenda of New Zealanders of European descent is conducted almost entirely in the English language and it has a good deal in common with the liturgical agenda of English-speaking descendants of European migrants in other parts of the world, notably in Australia, South Africa, and North America.

The religious affiliation of the population of Aotearoa New Zealand according to declaration in the national census is mainly Christian. Other religions are very small, but there is a notable proportion of people, 20% of the total population, who declare themselves to have no religion. The population percentages of the main Christian churches according to census figures are Anglican 22%, Presbyterian 16%, Catholic 15%, Methodist 4%, Baptist 2%.[1]

I am conscious that in cultural settings other than my own the Eucharist is in some cases very similar and in other cases very different from that most familiar to me. I am also conscious that

---

[1] These figures are from the last 1991 national census, and are taken from the *New Zealand Official Yearbook 1995*. Wellington: Statistics New Zealand, 1995.

within other traditions of the Christian church the Eucharist is again both very similar and very different. My reflections on issues in the symbolism of Eucharist and the solutions which I suggest are founded on the practice of Eucharist within the cultural and religious limitations of my own context. I offer them to Christians in other contexts as an invitation to consider whether these are also central issues in their own contexts and as possible solutions if they are. In any case I suggest that the central issues appear not in the practice of Eucharist in general, not in some common core of eucharistic tradition, not in some universal meaning of Eucharist, not in some basic scriptural origin, but in the quite particular celebrations of Eucharist by specific people in specific places and at specific times. It is toward the concrete symbolism of these quite particular instances of Eucharist that I wish to direct the reader's attention.

My own involvement in Eucharist for the last thirty years has been as a priest. This has involved me in the intricacies of planning and performance from the particular point of view of one who is a major player in the liturgy. A particularly valuable experience, however, was a period of about five years when I attended many Sunday liturgies of a variety of church denominations purely as an observer and ritual analyst. The combination of an engaged involvement in a particular liturgical role with a more objective and analytic observer standpoint has been a major contributor to the perspective I adopt here on eucharistic symbolism.

The selection of the five issues discussed in this book as the most central issues has not been entirely my own decision. Over several years some groups of people in Aotearoa New Zealand spent time reflecting on the results of a survey conducted in 1990 on the understanding and practice of Eucharist among members of Catholic religious congregations. One of the results of these reflections was the pinpointing of six priorities for future reflection and action. Five of these priorities make up the chapters of this book. The sixth priority concerned working toward an acceptance of differences among us in our practice of Eucharist. This book as a whole is intended as a contribution to the acceptance of differences in the sense that it attempts to set out the central issues as clearly as I am able and to show the reasons for one solution rather than another. If the reader cannot accept the solutions I propose, these solutions may still perhaps be acceptable as legitimate alternatives, or at least the point where we begin to differ may be clarified. At the very least I hope that these explanations may establish the point that alternatives to current practices may be considered seriously as neither mad nor malicious.

I propose then to deal here with five issues pinpointed in those group reflections and which I suggest as among the most important contemporary issues in our understanding and practice of Eucharist. These five issues make up the chapters of this book:

(1) shared liturgical leadership,
(2) inclusive language,
(3) the relevance of liturgical language,
(4) the inculturation of eucharistic symbols and calendar,
(5) with whom and how often to celebrate Eucharist.

These are not the only issues in the symbolism of Eucharist. I noted above that one of the problems in liturgical planning and performance can be a bewilderment over so many viewpoints and issues which all seem to take up more time than is available. The selection of these five issues for the chapters of this book is a deliberate attempt to focus specifically and tenaciously on only *some* issues, indeed on the ones which appear to be the most central, and to resist the continual temptations to add more and more issues to the list. Issues can be dealt with only if we are able to establish some priority among them. There is a point in discussion at which the priority of issues has to be fixed. After that point a reworking of priorities becomes simply an exercise in avoidance. For better or for worse, and allowing that at a future time or in another place other issues could be priorities, I have settled upon the above five issues as my resolute, perhaps even obdurate, focus for the purposes of this book.

I have followed a common format in the treatment of each of these issues:

(a) I attempt firstly to clarify and focus the issue.
(b) I then propose a way forward. This is a solution only in the immediate sense that it suggests the next step.
(c) I name some of the theological principles which underlie, or which are provoked by, taking the proposed way forward.
(d) I propose what taking this way forward will imply at the practical liturgical level.
(e) I indicate briefly the results of these changes in eucharistic symbolism for the life of the community outside and beyond its Eucharists.

The solutions, or the beginning of solutions, which I suggest in the following chapters are not just idealistic hopes. They are attempts in which someone somewhere, or some communities here and there, are already engaged. Hardly anyone, as far as I am aware, is attempting all these solutions all at once. I suggest in chapter 5 that one of the important and often neglected aspects of Eucharist is that it is a negotiation among the participants. Few communities have yet found the solutions to all these issues, but those who are sensitive to defects in their eucharistic symbols, and are willing to remedy them, are engaged in a process of negotiation which takes time and patience. Some communities have begun such negotiations in earnest, some scarcely seem to know where to begin.

Finally, it may be helpful here to make a distinction between liturgical reform and liturgical renewal. Liturgical *reform* in this context refers to the revision and alteration of official liturgical books, and therefore also of the liturgical rites which they authorize and control, according to principles established by church authority. Liturgical *renewal*, on the other hand, refers to the ongoing responsibility of all Christians for the ways they celebrate God's presence among them. The following chapters are concerned with issues of liturgical *renewal* which feed into and continue beyond the more confined issues of liturgical reform in the sense defined above. These chapters chart ways of engaging in this process.

Chapter 1

Shared Liturgical Leadership

The Issue

The liturgical renewals of the 1970s produced a new liturgical phenomenon which no one seems to have consciously intended. This is the phenomenon of the *priest-centered Eucharist*. It has become common now for the priest to face the congregation almost single-handedly: to welcome them, to pray most of the prayers on their behalf, to read the gospel, to preach, to proclaim the eucharistic prayer, to distribute communion, to make most announcements and notices, and to pray the final blessing. Normally now there are some other people, such as readers and communion assistants, who play brief parts which in some measure reduce the priest-centeredness of the Eucharist. Overall, though, the modern Eucharist remains very close to a single-handed effort by the priest interacting with the communal responses of the congregation. This is not just a rare extravagance but occurs repeatedly Sunday after Sunday, month after month, year in and year out in the same community.

Essentially what I have described here is the role of the priest as what is now called the liturgical *presider*. We should not belittle the considerable feat that is entailed in such live performance Sunday after Sunday, year in and year out, in the same community. But we do need to wonder just what we have ended up with and whether this is what the Eucharist is supposed to be.

There are some gifted modern actors who can hold an audience on their own for an hour or more. I doubt, however, that

7

there is any modern actor who would dare to give virtually the same performance to the *same* audience every week for a year or more. Liturgical presiders have had to develop their own strategies for coping with such impossible expectations.

One strategy is the *wooden puppet* approach which maximizes preoccupation with God located either in a sacred book or in the middle distance just above the congregation. This strategy avoids the distraction of mere human beings except when they have to be addressed directly. In this style of presiding the priest minimizes human contact with the congregation even while facing them. It is a looking without engagement, a talking to God in the presence of onlookers, an address without invitation. What has happened here is that an older style of liturgical leadership where priest and people *faced in the same direction* toward God located beyond the congregation, i.e., everyone faced the back of the person in front, has been carried over into a style of leadership where the *priest faces the people*. And when this happens the presider is exposed to the congregation in such a way as to appear distant, indifferent, or uncomfortable.

In a very different style of presiding, some priests work hard to overcome the formalism and privacy of the presiding style described above. They adopt a much more *interactive* approach. They project their own personalities into the role of presider, introduce personal reflections, and relate to the congregation in a more personalized way. This friendly informal approach maximizes smiling facial expression, eye contact with the congregation, and conversational address at appropriate points in the Eucharist ritual. It can take an extreme form where the Eucharist ritual is smothered beneath a kind of personality cult of the presider. In its milder forms, the more informal and personalized style is appreciated by many congregations.

This is a case, however, where the more you succeed the more you fail. The more successful the priest is at informalizing and personalizing the presider role, the more the Eucharist is made dependent upon the presider and the presider's own personality and personal gifts. That is to say, the more successful the priest is at this style of presiding, the more the Eucharist becomes *priest-centered*. The effectiveness of a Eucharist, then, has come to depend on the personality of the presider, and more particularly on that presider's acting and crowd-control skills.

The shift from the *ritual-centered* Eucharist where all participants were engaged in a standardized ritual form with minimum personal input, to the *priest-centered* Eucharist where the personality and performing ability of the priest became of central importance, was probably unanticipated in the liturgical reforms of the 1960s and 1970s. In hindsight, however, the priest-centered Eucharist can be seen to be a natural consequence of the concept of the mono-presider. And the *mono*-presider already had its basis in the mass-saying priest and the academic preacher of several centuries before.

What has been lost here is the sense that the assembly of believers is itself the active subject of the eucharistic liturgy. The priest has an important role within that active assembly, but it ought not to be the only important role. Many of the recent liturgical reforms were intended to increase the participation of the people in liturgy. But in a thoroughly priest-centered liturgy the rest of the assembly have become merely respondents. That is to say, their actions are dependent responses to the initiative of the mono-presider. A sense of the priesthood of all the faithful is still minimal here. But let us see if we can examine this issue in more detail.

Where precisely, then, does the phenomenon of the priest-centered Eucharist become an issue? It is an issue because it faces us with a choice. This choice appears at three levels:

The issue appears firstly in terms of *performance* as I have described it above. The priest-centered Eucharist depends to a large degree and in a most obvious way on the performing abilities of the priest, i.e., on the priest's talent at forms of talk, facial expression, and body language. Two points need to be made about such performance: (a) It requires an exposure to the congregation of the priest's own spirituality both in its depth and in its shallowness, in its authenticity and in its self-deceit. (b) Such performance must be producible on demand; that is to say, the regular Sunday (or daily) celebration of Eucharist has no respect for the times and rhythms of the priest's own spiritual life. There are few priests who would consciously want the Eucharist to be so dependent on the delicate and fragile texture of the priest's own spiritual life. Nevertheless, locked by the modern liturgy into single-handed face-to-face interaction with the congregation, the priest has to choose either for withdrawal into the wooden-puppet style or for the exposure of personalized performance, or for some kind of combination of both of these. Or, and worse, the priest is unaware that there is any conflict here and simply enjoys being the center of attention.

The priest-centered liturgy becomes an issue, then, in terms of *performance* because the expectations are impossible. The Eucharist becomes eventually disappointing to the congregation as the shallowness of the priest's spirituality becomes inevitably more and more exposed, and the priest's performance becomes tied into strategies which attempt to cope with the gap between performance and expectation.

Secondly, the priest-centered liturgy becomes an issue of *ministry* in more general terms because a priest-centered Eucharist means a priest-controlled Eucharist. Ministry in this form comes to be an expression or an exercise of dominance. The priest-centered Eucharist represents ideologies of control and submission, of producer and consumer. It is not the priest alone who is caught up in these patterns of control and submission. Control can be exercised by one person only if others submit. One person becomes a producer of grace only if others want to be consumers of grace. The priest-centered Eucharist is a symbol of a wider pattern and becomes an issue on the wider level of the nature of ministry in the church. It faces us with a choice of whether ministry becomes entangled in patterns of dominance and control or whether it is a specific contribution, a specific and limited service, within a larger pattern of participation of many people and many ministries within the community.

Thirdly, perhaps less obviously but even more seriously, the priest-centered Eucharist becomes an issue in its inadequate and distorted *representation of God*. The mono-presider, particularly when the same person presides weekly at the same assembly, will tend over a period of time to exclude understandings of God different from that of the presider. Eventually, for lack of opportunity, for lack of representation, most other presences of God in the community become disabled and disconnected from the community's Eucharist. The understanding of God expressed and present in those Eucharists eventually becomes narrowed to that of the priest's own spirituality. There are, of course, some counteracting forces to this within the liturgy itself. A variety of scriptural texts over time and the formal prayer texts of the liturgy itself expose people to a variety of images of God. But these are still channelled through the intonations and emphases of the priest's personal spirituality. Overall, other voices and other faces of God are likely to become silenced or veiled.

A Way Forward

A way forward is concerned essentially with some reduction of the activity of the presider and increased participation of the rest of the assembly. We may recall here that the action of the Eucharist is the action of the assembly as a whole rather than just the action of the presider. But a liturgical assembly is not just a mass of people acting in unison nor is it a collection of individuals acting at random. When I refer to the liturgical assembly "as a whole" I do not mean to imply that everyone in it is the same. It is internally structured. Briefly, sufficient for our purposes here, we may classify the structured roles within a eucharistic assembly under the headings of (a) *observers* (those physically present but psychologically distant from the liturgical action), (b) *participants only* (those whose engagement in the liturgy occurs through actions in common), (c) *ministers* (those who are "main actors" in a liturgy in that they not only do things *with* the other participants but actively do something *for* or *to* some or all of the other participants), (d) *recipients* (those toward whom the liturgical action is directed in some specific and explicit way).

I suggest that simply increasing the actions and common responses of the "participants only" is in itself insufficient to resolve the issue of the priest-centered Eucharist. This remains a minimal exercise of the priesthood of all believers. I do not suggest that this should not be done, but merely that we can already see it to be insufficient. We need to treat the assembly in a more refined and sophisticated fashion than as a uniform group of respondents in unison. I suggest rather that, beyond the "participants only," we should direct our attention to those roles in the structure of the liturgical assembly which I have classified above as "ministers." And I shall suggest later that within the "ministers" it is particularly the leadership roles that should claim our attention. Let me try to explain this suggestion step-by-step and in some more detail.

The first, most obvious, and easiest way to reduce the problem of the priest-centered Eucharist is to multiply ministries and ministers in the Eucharist. This means simply that instead of one person doing almost everything (a position of complete dominance or complete servitude depending on one's point of view), the actions within the Eucharist are carried out by a variety of people. This implies both (a) that we multiply the various ministerial roles within the Eucharist (readers, ministers of communion, ushers, announcers, those who say or lead prayers at various times, cantors, commentators, etc.), and (b) that we multiply the number of people who play each of these ministerial roles—we ensure that there are within any community a number of people capable of carrying out each of these ministerial roles. The multiplication of ministries within the Eucharist cannot of course be made at whim. They must be intrinsically and integrally derived from the Eucharist itself. This point need not delay us here since most communities have already made this move.

Few communities could be said to have taken these ministries seriously however. In few communities is there serious investment of time and money in educating people for these ministries.

In few communities is there substantial investment in investigating and implementing what these ministries *within* Eucharist imply for ministry in the community *outside* Eucharist. In only a few congregations are, for example, the people who read the scriptures during the Eucharist selected because they are the people most deeply engaged in meditation on and study of the scriptures, the people most skilled in proclaiming scripture effectively, and the people most capable of leading scripture study and discussion outside of Eucharist. Similarly for ministers of communion. The priest may have been sent to study for years before being permitted to play a leadership role in Eucharist, yet those who are "God-bearer" to others at communion are seldom trained in the theology of this ministry or its implications for that community outside the time of Eucharist. Similar comments apply to the hospitality role of ushers, those who pray the intercessions, and so on.

These ministries, even when not undertaken with any seriousness, do nevertheless relieve the monotony and monopoly of one person doing almost everything and nearly everyone else reduced to religious consumers. All the same, in most communities these ministers are treated as not strictly necessary. They are the priest's helpers rather than ministers in their own right. The move to introduce a variety of ministries in the Eucharist becomes a serious attempt to solve the problem of the priest-centered Eucharist only when the people performing these ministries have been trained and become expert in their own ministries. When undertaken seriously, rather than simply as priests' helpers, this multiplication of ministries and ministers reduces the problem of the priest-centered Eucharist.

In itself, however, a multiplication of ministries in Eucharist, does not address the issue of *leadership*. It does not solve the problem of the mono-presider even though it somewhat reduces the grosser effects of the priest-centered Eucharist. The extreme form of the priest-centered Eucharist is that where the priest is the (almost) sole actor doing (almost) all things except those done by the congregation in unison. In its reduced form with a multiplication of ministries, the priest-centered Eucharist is that where a mono-presider no longer does everything but is the supervisor in charge of everything and everyone.

In order to center on the issue of leadership, we will need here to make a distinction between the liturgical "leader" and the liturgical "minister." I use the term "minister" here to refer to a liturgical role with a specific task. Thus there may be "readers" whose specific role is to read the scriptures; "collectors" whose specific role is to collect the offerings and possibly also to present these in some formal ritual way; "ushers" whose specific role is to facilitate the gathering of people in the liturgical space; "communion ministers" whose specific role is to give communion; "musicians" whose specific role is the performing of music; etc. The term "ministry" may also refer to liturgical roles which have not yet received commonly agreed names or which are quite brief in duration such as the roles of those who proclaim the intentions for intercessory prayer, those who pray at particular times such as during the introductory rite. All these I refer to as "ministries."

These ministries are distinct on the one hand from simple participation expressed in communal responses, communal singing, communal movement, common posture. An increase in such ministries to an appropriate level has the positive effect of increasing participation beyond the level of common responses, increasing the possibilities of service within the community, increasing the opportunities for a variety of spiritual gifts. It has the purgative effect of decreasing in some degree the dominance of a mono-presider, and begins to free up slightly the mono-presider's narrowing of God. The implementation of a variety of ministries has been the first move in beginning to deal with the issue of the priest-centered Eucharist.

On the other hand, however, these ministries should not be confused with liturgical *leadership*. "Leadership" is a very specific kind of ministry which is not so much concerned with the performance of a particular action, but rather with the overall execution of the Eucharist ritual or some major part of it. The accent here is not on a particular action (reading, preaching, praying, collecting donations, ushering, giving communion, singing or playing music, etc.) but in facilitating, leading, and centering the liturgical performance.

It is only at the level of leadership that the issue of the mono-presider can be addressed directly and in an effective way. Ministries, of themselves, remain subsidiary or peripheral to the mono-presider. Unless the leadership issue itself is addressed, the problem of the priest-centered Eucharist with its performative inadequacy, its dominance of people, and its narrowing of God is only slightly reduced by an increased variety of other ministries.

The problem of the mono-presider once recognized as a problem has a simple solution. The solution is to increase the number of leadership roles. Again, these leadership roles cannot be multiplied simply at whim. Their number and kind must derive from the internal structure of the Eucharist itself. The ritual of the Eucharist has three main phases: the liturgy of the word, the liturgy of the Eucharist, and the liturgy of gathering and sending. Most people are familiar with the distinction between the liturgy of the word and the liturgy of the Eucharist within the overall Eucharist rite. The "liturgy of gathering and sending" perhaps needs some further explanation.

We are used to referring to the beginning and end of the Eucharist ritual as the "introductory rite" and the "concluding rite" or some similar terms. But it is of the nature of the Eucharist that it is not simply "introduced" and "concluded." The Eucharist can take place only when believers are gathered together in the name of Christ and in the power of the Spirit. They are not always nor automatically there. They have to gather there in such a way that they form a Christian assembly. They come from and are dispersed to other places and to a variety of daily lives. They do not simply go away. They are sent. They cannot stay in the place and time of Eucharist. They are sent away from it, commissioned to spread this power and this love to the lives from which they came and now return.

Eucharist is not simply introduced and concluded. Nor does it simply start and finish. Nor do people arrive there automatically and just carry on again as usual afterwards. They gather, and after gathering they are sent out again on God's mission to the world. It does not take much time for a leader to gather God's people and then later to send them out again, but it requires great skill. The liturgy of gathering and sending is as intrinsic and important to the Eucharist as are its other two main parts. Thus there are also three distinct (but not separate) leadership roles within the ritual process of Eucharist: leadership of the liturgy of the word, leadership of the liturgy of Eucharist, and leadership of the liturgy of gathering and sending.

The problem of the priest-centered Eucharist may be solved by the liturgical use of three leadership roles. These leadership roles do not supplant the already existing ministries within Eucharist. Each of the three leaders oversees and facilitates one of the three major phases of the Eucharist liturgy. What we have here is not a mono-presider, nor a leaderless liturgy, but a three-fold leadership pattern undertaken by three different people.

What Are the Theological Principles at Issue Here?

There is no suggestion here that in some simple way three is better than one. Nor is there any suggestion that three is again in some simple way more trinitarian than one. On the other hand, we should note that one is not somehow more godly nor more Christlike (representing Christ the head) than three either. Such arguments are often suggested and they should be discounted right from the start. Christo-monism is neither better nor worse than associating the triune God of Christianity with every appearance of the number three. There is no general sense in which one is liturgically better than three, nor any general sense in which three is liturgically better than one.

More seriously, the theological issues which appear liturgically as the issue of the priest-centered Eucharist may be summarized as issues to do with (1) the organization of the church, (2) the force of tradition, and (3) our imagining of God.

(1) Church organization.

The liturgical mono-presider reflects a monarchical model of church organization, i.e., one pastor or priest or minister in charge of or leading the local community. A liturgical three-leadership model proposes a different model of community leadership, namely a model of team leadership overseeing and supporting a variety of more specialized ministries. The theological principles involved here are not merely liturgical but affect, too, the rest of community organization. The model of the one pastor-in-charge is put in dispute here. Similarly in dispute are some of the more directly christological models of ministry which envisage the pastor or priest as "head" of the body in the way Christ is head of the church. This "head" theology (or *alter Christus* theology) of ministry and priesthood is here resisted by a more varied and cooperative model of leadership where no one person nor one ministry can play the role of Christ to the exclusion of other ministries. Some people fear that the only alternative to such "head" theology of ministry is a "headless" church. What is proposed here however is not a leaderless church, but neither is it a monarchical church. It is a church organization based on a variety of ministries supported and coordinated by a small leadership team.

The liturgical model does not spell out how this team leadership will work out in detail, for the Eucharist does not function as a direct and simple point-for-point working model of the life of the community. There are factors other than liturgical which determine the needs of community organization. Currently, however, the attempts at more cooperative and collaborative styles of leadership are in conflict with the mono-presider style of eucharistic liturgy. The public presentation and sanctioning of leadership at the community's most important gathering, namely its Sunday Eucharist, is a major influence on how that community functions outside Eucharist. At issue here, then, is not just our understanding of Eucharist but our understanding of Christian ministry, and especially leadership, within the Christian community.

The shift from the mono-presider to a three-leader pattern of leadership in Eucharist demonstrates a shift in power within the church community. This needs to be noticed because some will favor or oppose liturgical change on the basis of their attitudes to power. Moreover, such a liturgical shift suggests that one person cannot adequately represent God to others. Hence leadership within the church community would require a team or college of persons rather than one single individual.

(2) The force of tradition.

A second theological issue concerns the value we place on tradition. The currently popular mono-presider remains in liturgical continuity with the traditional monarchist model of Eucharist leadership. Are we prepared to abandon this tradition in favor of a model with three leadership roles?

Let us note firstly that the mono-presider is not quite as traditional as it may first appear. We do not know precisely how Eucharists were celebrated in the first-century church, but the variety of ministerial and leadership styles in the New Testament make a widespread use of a mono-presider in Eucharist unlikely. The single bishop with a group of presbyters and deacon assistants which seems to have been quite widespread by the third century is still a different model from that of the mono-presider. The mono-presider model develops out of the sole-actor model (the priest who "says" mass with or without congregation) which became common during the European early Middle Ages. The immediate predecessor of our modern priest-centered Eucharist was the "low mass" with its sole-actor, rather than the more official though less common "high mass" with its variety of ministers. Thus the mono-presider model cannot claim to represent a constant and widespread tradition. But it can trace a fairly direct pedigree back through the "low mass" to the medieval sole-actor model. And it has somewhat more complex connections with the role of the bishop in the patristic Eucharist.

A more collaborative approach to liturgical leadership can trace its connections back through the varied liturgical roles of the "high mass," the more complex bishop-presbyters-deacons model of the patristic Eucharist and the varied ministries of its catechumenate, to the earlier group presbyterate and the just barely glimpsed liturgical roles of teachers, prophets and apostles of the early church.

More important perhaps and more fundamental than the pedigree of the mono-presider on the one hand, or collaborative leadership on the other, is the value we attach to continuity or discontinuity in tradition. No church claims that we should never change anything from the way it was done in the church of the apostles. No one values tradition absolutely for then our Eucharists would be in all respects the same as that of the original thanksgiving meals of Jesus with his disciples, or at least of the first post-resurrection Christian communities. This is not only not the case with any modern Eucharist, it could not possibly be the case because we do not know very much about what those first Eucharists were like. The older centers of Christianity may quite properly place considerable value on the continuity of their own tradition. And for this reason they may be reluctant to introduce changes of any sort until they have been proven necessary and their continuity with tradition can be clearly seen.

The newer local churches at the "ends of the earth" may however take a different view. Change and discontinuity are always necessary because Christian tradition so far has been developed in foreign places and foreign cultures. Any simple copy of traditional Christianity is culturally and spiritually alienating for the more recent local churches. In such places, a local Christianity has to be in some degree new and in discontinuity with the traditional Christian past. This means that anything which claims to be part of Christian "tradition" has to be examined for the degree to which it is simply a past inculturation of Christianity in a foreign culture. It is difficult to argue that the sole-actor model, the bishop-presbyters-deacons model, or the three-leader model are any more or less one than the other cultural adaptations of the New Testament Eucharist.

The second theological principle at issue here then is that of the relative value we place on tradition or inculturation. As far as the churches of the South Pacific are concerned, all traditions are foreign inculturations of Christianity and therefore subject to some degree of change. There is no obvious reason why the cultural models of the second or third century Mediterranean world should be better, or more divine or more godly or more Christian than those of the twentieth-century South Pacific. The same may be said for the churches of Asia, of sub-Saharan Africa, and of the Americas.

Two important points remain in this consideration of tradition and inculturation. (a) Whatever the origins of the mono-presider model, it is a model of leadership which people have become accustomed to within church communities. Any change to that custom has to take into account the way in which Eucharist acts as a marker of identity and we have to be careful lest any change in Eucharist may be an act of disenfranchisement for some people who have identified with a traditional leadership model. At the same time, (b) customary practices are not politically neutral in the contemporary world. The mono-presider model resonates with contemporary experience of, for example, patriarchal household models, kingship models, military, industrial, and academic models where one person is in charge of and has power over others. These are line-management and hierarchical models which differ markedly from other contemporary models such as leadership in sports clubs and voluntary associations, two-parent households, business and professional partnerships, producer and consumer cooperatives, team management. A liturgical decision for a mono-presider model on the one hand or a team leadership model on the other is not just an act of faithfulness to a selected tradition, it is also taking a political option within the contemporary world.

(3) Images of God.

Eventually, most important of all are the images of God which are displayed in Eucharist. This is the most fundamental theological issue underlying the issue of the priest-centered Eucharist. The priest-centered Eucharist narrows the images of God in a way which over a period of time may become thoroughly distorting.

Images of God are presented to the assembly in many ways: the words by which God is addressed in prayer, the images contained in the scripture readings, the presentations of God in the homily, the ways in which people treat and acknowledge one another (in gesture, stance, movement as well as words), the attitudes of reverence and participation, the music, the pictorial representations. What concerns us in particular here though is the way in which the liturgical leader presents images of God to the rest of the assembly. The liturgical leader affects the presentation of God within the liturgy in four main ways. (i) The first of these derives directly from the leader's personal spirituality. The leader appears as one who is close to God and who knows about God, and therefore becomes a source of the knowledge of God for the congregation. But the personal spirituality of one person is always limited. If one person is constantly the leader of Eucharist over a long period of time, the images of God through this particular channel become inevitably limited. (ii) Closely related to the liturgical leader's personality but worth independent notice is the leader's actual performance during liturgy. Images of God presented within, for example, prayers and gestures of respect can be muted, exaggerated, highlighted, passed over, made to flourish or rendered unintelligible by the performance of the leader. Or conversely, images of God which do not occur in the prayer texts nor the formal gestures may be introduced or never occur at all depending on the imaginative and performing ability of the leader. The limitations of one leader's performing ability can be compensated for by other leaders, but a single leader is likely to become caught over time in a downward spiral of narrowing images of God.

(iii) A liturgical leader is not just a performer but also enables and controls the performances of other ministers. The leader is involved then in the planning and the creation of expectations for the overall liturgy, not just the leader's own performing parts within it. Again here the single leader's own limitations or personal discomfort with certain images may gradually eliminate over time the images of God which could otherwise have occurred in the actions or words of other ministers. Multiple leadership helps to counteract this effect. (iv) Beyond personal spirituality and personal skills, the liturgical leader is already socialized into and classified by the social definitions prominent in society and church such as gender, class, culture, educational level, and age. Each of these classifications has its own priorities and preferences in its understanding of God. A single leader again narrows the presentation of God in accordance with that leader's own place within society and church while multiple leadership is more likely to broaden that presentation.

Ultimately, this argument against the narrowing and distorting of the images of God is the most serious argument for a multi-ministry and multi-leadership model for Eucharist. And this argument is immeasurably reinforced when criteria for ordination to priesthood restrict that priesthood to celibate males. But even where priesthood (and therefore those who may be presiders) is restricted neither to males nor to celibates, the widening and varying of those who present images of God to the congregation remains an argument for multiple leadership in Eucharist. Those who argue for the mono-presider model of leadership need to overcome this most basic of defects in the priest-centered Eucharist.

What Are the Practical Liturgical Effects?

What effect does this three-leader model have on the actual performance of liturgy? Do we have here a three-headed monster clumsily dividing the unity of Eucharist represented by the mono-presider? Or, on the other hand, does this three-leader model mean simply a couple of changes of guard with everything else pretty much the same as before, an academic formality but really business as usual?

If we accept in principle a three-leader model of Eucharist, what effect does this have on the actual liturgical performance? The three-leader model does not imply that the three leaders are equal, equivalent or interchangeable. It is not a matter of three being better than one. Each phase of the Eucharist has its own meaning, style, and leadership requirements. Let us take each of these leadership roles in turn. For the purposes of detailed description I shall refer here to the current order of the Roman missal. Other orders of service will differ in details but the principles will be the same.

The leader of the *liturgy of the word* takes over formal leadership at the first scripture reading and concludes with the prayers of intercession. Leadership here involves both preparation before and performance during that Eucharist. Leadership requires seeing that all goes well, that all is prepared, that other ministers know which parts they play, that accidents are coped with, that each part moves surely into the next; it attends to cuing in the creed and the prayers of intercession. It is appropriate, too, that the leader of the word introduces the readings if necessary and delivers the homily, though these parts may sometimes be played by others. The leader needs to be visibly prominent during the liturgy of the word but the main role may be one of preparation and timing. This leadership role cannot be played by anyone at all. It requires thorough understanding of scripture and the skills of liturgical leadership. It further requires an ability to articulate the resonances of the word of God in the contemporary life of the community.

The leader of the *liturgy of the Eucharist* begins formal leadership at the preparation of gifts and concludes with the distribution of communion. This role requires leadership of the eucharistic prayer prayed in dialogue with the congregation. It also requires involvement, though usually with others, in the elaborate gestural language of attention to the gifts of bread and wine which form an integral part of the liturgy of the Eucharist. When required it is appropriate that this leader initiate or conclude actions and prayers surrounding the eucharistic prayer and the communion such as the exchange of peace and the showing of the eucharistic bread and wine to the congregation before individual reception.

The liturgy of the Eucharist is one of thanksgiving and unity. Its leader needs to be a person who can achieve this. Normally then, this person will be one officially ordained to this leadership. But most particularly the person required for this role in one who is involved in the community in such a way that he or she can in fact pray in thanksgiving and unity in dialogue with and on behalf of that assembly. This accent on unity, an accent on what this assembly has in common despite other differences, stands in contrast with the liturgy of the word where a much wider range of relationships are commonly required—confrontation, criticism, conversion as well as encouragement, gratitude, etc. The liturgy of the Eucharist unites in what is held in common, even when the liturgy of the word has uncovered a community split in disagreement, a community of sinners, a community of wide differences.

The leader of the *liturgy of gathering and sending* begins the formal role at whatever point it becomes possible for one person to begin the process of gathering others. This leader is essentially and literally responsible for the gathering, the assembling of the community. The ritual of gathering begins at the point when people begin to encounter one another, i.e., well before the first hymn or the first formal words of the leader. There is a point in time when these people are disparate and a point when they constitute an assembly. This gathering liturgy can vary a good deal. It may be quite simple and brief or more expanded. Where it is simple, the leader alone may be the only minister playing a part, though in a large congregation it is normally quite difficult to accomplish this without musicians at least. Where it is more expanded, a variety of other ministers may also take part. The leader needs to be careful here, though, that this gathering ritual does not go beyond its purpose and turn into a mini liturgy of the word.

The second half of this part of the liturgy, namely the liturgy of sending, is intimately related to gathering. The sending is usually quite simple and requires great skill, though with extreme caution it may sometimes be more elaborate. The essential element of the liturgy of sending is that some central strands which relate this celebration of Eucharist to the world from which these people come be focused in final prayers, blessings, gestures, and movements. Thus the leadership of gathering and sending articulates the relationship of this assembly to the world from which these people come and to which they return.

The requirements for leadership in this phase of the Eucharist are partly the liturgical skills to accomplish such an articulation. More importantly, however, and quite differently from the other two leadership roles, the leader of gathering and sending should thoroughly belong in the *place* in which the Eucharist is celebrated. In order to gather others, one must first be there in that place. In order to send others, one must continue in that place when others have gone. In some sense this leadership role is one of hospitality. Only those who are integrally part of this place can welcome others into it, establish the rules by which this gathering takes place—define in fact the identity of this assembly, and then send them back renewed to the places from whence they came, but retaining the identity of *this* place as one to which they will again return.

The requirements for each of these leadership roles are different. They are not equivalent nor interchangeable nor uniformly recruited. Each of these styles of leadership is different one from the other. There are different reasons why one person will be more suitable than another for any one of them.

Where the congregation is small these three leaders do not require much ritual marking as long as they can be clearly seen and heard. As the size of the congregation becomes bigger the ritual signs will normally need to be larger and clearer (clearly marked position in space, view of the whole congregation, special clothing, some special visual symbol, etc.). In general the larger the gathering, the more symbolically marked the leadership needs to be.

Beyond Liturgy

When we look beyond liturgy for post-liturgical effects we are looking for the transformative effects of the divine life on the participants. This divine life is communicated in the communicative actions among the participants in the Eucharist. The various ministers, and particularly the leaders, within the Eucharist ritual play a major part in this communicative action.

Firstly, the three leadership roles in Eucharist help to obviate the central fault in the mono-presider and the priest-centered Eucharist, namely, the narrowing of God. For what the liturgical leader is primarily about is God's communication with the participants. The self-expression of the leader in words, gestures, facial expression, movement, etc., reveals attitudes, beliefs, qualities, and spiritualities to the other participants. An increase in the number of ministers and a threefold leadership pattern, provided these grow organically and holistically from within the Eucharist ritual, have the effect of reversing the priest-centered Eucharist's tendency to narrow the community's imagining, understanding, and search for God.

Secondly, the Eucharist provides a model for the organization of the Christian community. A three-leadership pattern along with high participation of other ministries within the Eucharist signals the desirability of (where it does not exist), or reinforces (where it already exists) a participative and collegial community organization. Thus a team leadership approach to local church organization is encouraged by a parallel leadership pattern in that community's Eucharists. A team approach in church organization is almost impossible when that pattern is constantly contradicted in the community's Eucharists.

Thirdly, because each of the leadership roles in Eucharist has a different and more specialized function than the catch-all, do-everything mono-presider, each of these leaders can pay more attention to particular aspects of the relationship between the Eucharist and the rest of the community's life. It is particularly (but not solely) the leader of the gathering and sending rite who articulates the thresholds between the Eucharist assembly and the daily life of the community. It is also this leader as "host" at the place where the community assembles for Eucharist who (together with those others who play this role at other times, for this role is not played by one person all the time) pays careful attention to who is comfortable here, who is at home here, who is being excluded, who is abusing the hospitality of God's place, who is not yet but needs to be made welcome. But this leader (with others over time) is also careful that those who come here do not simply rest secure here, that the ethics of the non-liturgical world to which they return have been highlighted and somehow more sharply delineated in the liturgical world of the Eucharist.

Similarly, the leader of the liturgy of the Eucharist will pay much more careful attention to the nature of the thanksgiving and the unifying force of the eucharistic prayer and communion— unifying for this contemporary local community, between this and other contemporary communities, and between this contemporary community and its tradition. The leader of the liturgy of the word (along with those others who at different times play this same role) will ensure that the word of God is a living word in the lives of the community. One of the requirements here is that the homily is not confined within the spirituality of the mono-presider, but reflects wider spiritualities. And to ensure above all that it is not trapped within a minister or priest who has a role to play but nothing to say.

Chapter 2

Inclusive Language

The Issue

The issue of inclusive language centers most acutely around (a) *gender*-inclusive language, and (b) *culture*-inclusive language. I use the term "language" in this context to refer to *speech* only. I do not use it in this chapter, then, in the wider sense in which gesture, posture, movement and so on may be said to constitute a "body language," nor in the sense in which symbolic systems in general constitute a language.

Let me begin with the issue of *gender*-inclusive language. Let us agree firstly that a person's gender is not a valid Christian criterion for exclusion from the Christian community. Any action then which tends to exclude on the basis of gender has no place in Eucharist. Part of the problem with liturgical language is that some liturgical speakers, both women and men, continue to regard specifically masculine terms ("man," "he," "his," etc.) as both masculine and gender-free, i.e., as including women *sometimes*. Since, however, this is widely rejected in almost all areas of public writing and speaking in our society, I do not propose to reenter this old debate here. For our purposes here, I shall assume that in modern English usage "man," "he," "his," and similar words refer to males only. They are not neutral, they are not inclusive, and they have all sorts of social, political, and economic effects mainly centered around issues of power and normality.

Even where there is an acceptance in principle that such language is not inclusive of women, the issue of gender-inclusive language in liturgy still remains problematic. As a specifically liturgical issue, it may be further pinpointed as follows:

(1) While we may agree on the need for gender-inclusive *people* language, there remains the issue of gender-inclusive *God* language. May we continue to refer to God as if God were masculine? May we continue to refer to God as "Father" or as "Lord"? Or if we do so are we required then to create a balance by the use of some specifically feminine terms to refer to God? Or should we use only words with no specific gender reference such as Creator, Savior, Wisdom, Source of all life, Spirit, Word?

(2) Since much liturgical language has traditionally been exclusive of women, we are involved here not simply in producing in a vacuum, so to speak, the most gender-inclusive set of words, but of *change* from customary words to new words. And intrinsic to the issue of change is that of (a) *who* makes the changes, and (b) how much community *agreement* there should be, for agreement is rarely total, before these changes are made, i.e., how tyrannical or consensual the process of change should be.

Let us leave the question of gender-inclusive language for the time being and attempt in a similar way to pinpoint the issues involved in culture-inclusive language. In the case of culture-inclusive language, the issue is rather different. We must again select a starting point. I shall assume that, as for gender, so also culture does not constitute a legitimate criterion for exclusion from the Christian community. I shall assume, too, that the language of the Eucharist should be the language of the participants. Again here I am concerned solely with the case of speech and not with any other kind of cultural symbols.

Culture-inclusive language becomes an issue when the participants at Eucharist are made up of several primary language groups. The relationships between several cultures, several language groups, in the same place is never politically neutral. Hence the language or languages spoken in Eucharist indicate inclusion and exclusion, superiority and inferiority, normality and peripherality, among the cultures which make up this Christian community. In its decisions about culture-inclusive language, the genuine catholicity of the community is put to the test. The Christian community's identity, its boundaries of inclusion and exclusion, are here at issue.

The more precise nature of the issue may be pinpointed here by listing some often adopted positions which should *not* constitute a solution, i.e., some attractive non-solutions, namely, (1) the "all-inclusive" solution, (2) the "worth-doing-badly" solution, (3) the "majority-rules" solution, (4) the "first-here" solution.

(1) The *all-inclusive* solution is at first sight the most attractive. If cultural exclusiveness contradicts the catholicity of Eucharist, why not just include everyone? If only two language groups are present, then this may indeed be a solution though it requires great skill and effort not to subordinate one language to the other and to maintain proportion. Where there are more than two language groups present then any attempt at an all-inclusive solution is likely to result in chaos or tokenism. The greater the number of language groups the more impossible this solution becomes. The simple all-inclusive solution is possible in very few cases under very limited conditions. As a general solution it is likely to cause more problems than it solves. Some judgments need to be made about ritual coherence and unity, the problems of tokenism, the relative number of participants in each language group, the possibility of different solutions at different times, and the already existing political inequalities among language groups.

(2) The *worth-doing-badly* solution may be regarded as a variant of the all-inclusive solution. It takes the stand that the variety of languages should be acknowledged even if this is done badly. This means that various parts of the Eucharist are allotted to the various languages represented within the community. Whereas the all-inclusive solution is attractive in theory but usually chaotic in practice, this solution proposes that we should go

ahead anyway. This position puts high value on the liturgical acknowledgement of language groups. Its weakness lies often in its inattention to how difficult it is to do this well and it hovers on the borders of tokenism. In one sense a "token" may be a simple and gracious recognition of people and their value by public recognition of their language. In the pejorative sense, "tokenism" refers to the failure to achieve this goal, as, for example, when (a) an incompetent speaker mangles the language so that it is silly or embarrassing or insulting to native speakers; (b) the language token is tediously repetitive or incoherent with the rest of the liturgy so that it is awkward for or patronizing toward that language group; (c) the language token has no implementation in the non-liturgical life of the community.

(3) The *majority-rules* solution proposes that the liturgy be conducted in the language of the majority of the participants or in the language understood by the greatest number of participants. This is, in my experience, the most commonly adopted solution. This solution is attractive because it seems to be the most democratic and it satisfies the greatest number of people. It is not, however, a satisfactory liturgical solution because it belittles language minorities. It either ignores them completely or it requires them to assemble separately in their own language-based Eucharist. This solution is particularly objectionable in Eucharist if the principle of majority rule already operates in the society at large, so that language minorities have no voice either in society or in the church's Eucharists.

(4) The *first-here* solution proposes that the culture which is first in that place provides the language for the Eucharists of that local church. This solution has the advantage that it makes a stand for the indigenous language in the case where this is endangered. But it requires migrant language groups to abandon their own language in order to participate in Eucharist. Because of the huge reality of migration in the modern world this solution may also reduce effective communication in

Eucharist when the indigenous language is understood by only a minority of participants.

Each of the above-described attempts at culture-inclusive language has some attractive element but none constitutes a solution on its own. We will need to look for a solution which is able to cope with greater complexity than any of these simple first-sight solutions.

A Way Forward

Let us deal firstly with the issue of inclusive *gender* language. I propose here that we set out to move from sexist liturgical language toward gender-inclusive language by way of four recognitions which provide the stepping stones for this advance.

(1) *God is not specifically male and our God language should not indicate or imply therefore that God is male rather than female.*

I have assumed here an agreement that "people" language, i.e., language about human beings, is to be gender-inclusive. I further assume though, since this is the case in most eucharistic communities with which I am familiar, that our "God" language is more difficult to change—as a community we are not quite sure how much change should be made, nor altogether clear what we should change to. Nevertheless we are agreed, I again assume, that God is not male nor female. Gender-inclusive God language arises as an issue because of the dislocation which occurs when we believe in a God who is neither female nor male, or is as well female as male, but our language commonly refers to that God in masculine terms.

(2) *The change to gender-inclusive God language is a participative process rather than a single once-for-all decision.*

Some eucharistic communities can make rapid and radical changes in their customary ways of referring to, thinking about, and speaking about God. These are usually small communities which spend a good deal of time together working through matters which concern them. Most eucharistic communities, however, will need to deal with such change in a series of steps. The cost of not taking such steps over a period of time is likely to be an act of tyranny by community leaders or by blocs within that community. The image of God portrayed in such acts may be as idolatrous as the sexist images of God which they seek to eliminate. The change to gender-inclusive language does not need to be achieved by acts of power and conquest. Nor however does it need to wait for complete consensus at the pace of the most recalcitrant member of the community. An agreement on gender-inclusive language can be achieved in a series of steps where there is time and opportunity for legitimation or alteration at each step.

(3) *The process of change towards gender-inclusive God language is shaped by two important factors affecting liturgical language: (a) the responsibility for liturgical speeches, and (b) the sacredness of liturgical texts.*

A Eucharist liturgy is not controlled totally by one person, nor is it controlled simply by the community as a whole. The eucharistic liturgy belongs primarily to the community which gathers regularly to celebrate Eucharist. But the various speech segments of a liturgy are normally delegated to particular liturgical roles within that community. The people playing these roles are responsible for their effective implementation, i.e., for consistency and variation of spoken words within the limits that the community can accept. Moreover, the speech segments within the liturgy have varying degrees of "sacredness" attached to them. As a general principle, the more sacred are the words spoken during a liturgy, the more the words will be controlled by a written text. The more sacred these texts, i.e., the more central to the community's traditional identity, the more they resist modern change.

(4) *The struggle itself is worthwhile.*

When dealing with liturgical language we are always concerned with a workable degree of community agreement rather than merely tolerance, passive acceptance, or passive resistance at the purely liturgical level. It is the community negotiation itself that is the vital issue here, rather than a decision by particular individuals to use gender-inclusive liturgical language. The issue needs to be negotiated, i.e., engaged in and worked through at the symbolic level, in order for it to change attitudes and behavior outside of and beyond the liturgy.

With these four recognitions we are in a position to look in more detail at each of the two important factors in liturgical language which I have proposed above: (a) the *responsibility* for liturgical speeches, and (b) the *sacredness* of liturgical texts. In effect, a eucharistic community will find a way forward toward gender-inclusive language by utilizing these two factors. Non-recognition of these two factors is likely to result in both personal frustration and communal chaos.

When people are given *responsibility for liturgical speeches*, there is implied a duty to ensure adequate performance as well as some right to control and vary that performance. The following delegations of responsibility are fairly common: the hymns are decided by a liturgy committee or music leader, the readers of scripture are a limited number of selected and trained people, an ordained priest leads the eucharistic prayer, a pastoral worker is responsible for the prayers of intercession, the bulletin writer has responsibility for notices, the homilist is responsible for the homily. These are only the most obvious ones. They may differ from congregation to congregation and only some of them are formally written into official rubrics.

The important point to recognize here is that linguistic change in the Eucharist occurs not simply by the decision of a central authority, nor simply by a referendum of the whole community, but through the complex web of responsibilities for liturgical speeches which regulate community liturgy. This is daunting only for the outsider. The regular participant in a community's Eucharists is already familiar with most of this web of responsibility. A conscious recognition of who is responsible for what simplifies considerably the processes of change and clarifies the legitimate limitations to change.

The second significant aspect of liturgical language that concerns us here is that of the *sacredness of liturgical texts*. The most easily altered liturgical speeches are those for which there are no written texts or whose texts are personally generated, e.g., the homily, spontaneous prayers, various kinds of brief instructions and invitations to the congregation. Some of the speech segments of a liturgy, however, are constrained by written texts, e.g., biblical texts, some formal liturgical prayers. A written text is not itself part of the liturgical speech, but it controls liturgical speech. The more sacred a text is, that is, the more central it is to the community's identity and faith, the more it is resistant to contemporary alteration.

Four kinds of texts need to be taken into consideration here: (i) hymns, (ii) authorized modern liturgical texts, (iii) traditional credal texts, (iv) biblical texts. A common condition of these texts is that their ownership lies (with very few exceptions) outside of the eucharistic community. Any alteration of these texts gives rise to issues which are somewhat different for each of these four kinds of texts. Briefly these issues are as follows:

(i) Many hymns have been written by modern writers and any alteration involves respect for the original creative act of the lyricist, the interests of the publisher, and the more legal issues of copyright.

(ii) Authorized modern liturgical texts usually have their origin in a central church authority outside the eucharistic community. Such texts may be, for example, the eucharistic prayers, collect prayers, blessing formulae. The speaker of these texts may find conflict between what is appropriate within this particular eucharistic community and what has been authorized. These texts as authoritative are resistant to change. But this resistance is relative since it is known that they have been and may again be altered by some contemporary authority within the church.

(iii) More resistant to change are traditional credal texts such as the Apostles' Creed, the Nicene Creed, the traditional trinitarian endings of formal prayers. Such traditional texts themselves constrain rather than depend upon contemporary church authority. Since the original authors themselves cannot change such texts, they seem to be unchangeable (though of course their translations may change). They may perhaps be quietly abandoned or the frequency of their use be simply reduced, but it is much more difficult to actually change them since their ownership is well beyond any claim of a contemporary eucharistic community.

(iv) Finally, the biblical texts are the texts most of all resistant to change. Their origin as divinely inspired seems to put them out of reach of the contemporary eucharistic community. They are so central to Christian liturgy that they cannot be quietly abandoned nor even their frequency reduced. Particularly significant among biblical texts are those which are not only read but which are also memorized and have become integral to Christian prayer—in particular the baptismal formula (Father, Son, and Holy Spirit) and the "Our Father." (But again, of course, their translations may change.)

What I want to establish at this point is that the process of participative change toward gender-inclusive language includes a recognition of these two factors: the delegation of responsibility for liturgical speeches, and the sacredness of liturgical texts. The recognition of these factors in liturgical communication shows us the bones of a participative process which is an alternative between complete frustration on the one hand and destructive acts of power on the other.

I have left the details of how these recognitions may be worked out in practice to a later section dealing with practical effects. Let me turn again now to the issue of *culture*-inclusive language and seek a way forward for that part of the liturgical language issue.

The issue of culture-inclusive language does not admit of one simple solution since (a) the number of language groups within local communities may vary from one to dozens, (b) the relationships between those language groups in society may be politically complex (histories of conflict or harmony, economic unfairness or dependence, political oppression, legal or social discrimination, etc.). Hence, a way forward must be sought not so much in a proposed process of change (as was possible in the case of *gender*-inclusive language), but by suggesting the principles which guide the way to satisfactory solutions.

I suggest that, although each combination of language groups constituting a local eucharistic community will need to find its own particular solution, the process for reaching a culture-inclusive solution will require a consideration of six elements. These are (1) *which* languages are to be spoken, (2) *what* is said, (3) *who* says it, (4) *how often* those languages are spoken, (5) *where* they are spoken, and most fundamentally (6) who *decides*.

(1) Which languages:

In trying to focus the issue more closely I have already suggested that we avoid some attractive non-solutions, in particular, the all-inclusive solution, the majority-rules solution, the first-here solution, the worth-doing-badly solution. Although these, each on its own, are non-solutions, they remain attractive because each contains some element which may contribute to a genuine solution. The all-inclusive and the worth-doing-badly solutions recognize, one idealistically the other more practically, that liturgy is not simply neutral in the relationships between language groups and cultures, that the liturgical ignoring of a language group may be an act of cultural domination. The majority-rules solution recognizes the necessity of coherence and intelligibility in liturgy. The first-here solution recognizes the value of indigenous languages without which Christianity would deny its professed universality.

The decision on *which* languages should be included in a community's Eucharist depends in large manner on two factors: non-liturgical use and the recognition of political inequality.

(a) The non-liturgical use of a language. Not all the primary languages of the people normally present at a regular Eucharist can or need be spoken during a community's Eucharist. In many modern Christian communities this would reduce the Eucharist to incoherence. The fact that a language is spoken by some individuals or within some families who normally participate in a Eucharist does not of itself make a claim for liturgical recognition. It is when that language moves beyond family or cultural usage and becomes used in a specifically Christian-identified grouping that it requires liturgical recognition in that community's Eucharists. When a language is used by a Christian group in their non-eucharistic gatherings, it then has serious claims for recognition and usage within the community's Eucharists.

(b) The recognition of political inequality. The use of language in a community's Eucharists takes place within a larger political and ethical setting. Cultures are not politically equal in society. Equality in Eucharist is something to be striven for against the background of the current inequalities among the cultures in that society. There is a temptation for Eucharist to replay the discriminations already existing in society. Thus a dominant language group in society may tend to dominate also in Eucharist. A eucharistic community will need to make special efforts to resist this, so that their Eucharists are a contribution to cultural equality and catholicity within the Christian church.

It is a mistake, however, to imagine that we need to pay attention only to which language is spoken. The two factors of non-liturgical use and political inequality go some way to indicating the direction of culture-inclusive language, but clearly they are not in themselves sufficient.

(2) What is said:

Once we have come to a decision that certain languages have a serious claim to inclusion in our Eucharist, this is still not yet a liturgical decision. Or rather, it is only part of a *liturgical* decision. The question is not solved by scattering languages at random through a Eucharist nor by treating all speech segments as equal. A liturgical decision includes a decision on which particular speech segments are to be spoken in which particular language. Some languages may have a better claim than others on some parts of the Eucharist ritual in the sense that they have a better cultural contribution to make there. Some languages groups, for example, already have powerful rituals of welcome, some have strong oratorical traditions which parallel the style of the eucharistic prayer, some have customs of spontaneous prayer. Other language groups have relatively dull alternatives to those particular speech segments. Or again, a liturgical issue in one language may simply not occur in another. The non-inclusive trinitarian formula (Father, Son, Holy Spirit) in English, for example, simply does not occur in some other languages whose familiar trinitarian formulae are already gender-inclusive (e.g., equivalent in English to "Parent," "Child," Holy Spirit).[1] *What* is said, in other words, is not simply interchangeable from one language to another. Thus, some speech segments may be more ritually rich in the customs and oratory of one language than of others. *What* is said needs then to be taken into consideration over and above the decision on which languages should occur during a Eucharist.

Two further points, though important, may be made here quite briefly because they are reasonably obvious. The first is that a dominant language may establish its dominance not simply by excluding other languages but also by treating all other languages as additions, as optional extras, rather than more valuable alternatives. Care needs to be taken here then that speech segments in one language are not simply repeated in another language, except where repetition is already integral to that speech segment (as in the case of litanies and some forms of intercessory prayer). The second point is that there are some

---

[1] Some Eucharist leaders in Aotearoa New Zealand, for example, use trinitarian formulae in the indigenous Maori language for blessings, whatever the language of the rest of the Eucharist. This is partly because it recognizes the indigenous status of Maori and partly because in Maori (as distinct, for example, from English) this formula is already and traditionally gender-inclusive.

speech segments of the Eucharist where, because that segment is common to all or most Eucharists, the congregation already knows what is going on even if they do not understand the language in which that segment is spoken. Such segments are more available than others for language substitution without resulting in unintelligibility.

When we pay attention then to *what* is said we are doing two things. First, we are simply completing the liturgical decision which includes not only *which* languages will be spoken but also decisions about *what particular speech segments* will be spoken in this or that language. Second, we are going beyond the simple *acknowledgement* of language groups as constituting part of the eucharistic community and recognizing that languages are not simply interchangeable. We are recognizing here that a particular language may have its own particular liturgical value which another language does not have. We are recognizing, too, that what is said in one language may not be the same as what is said in another language even though in translation it seems virtually the same because (a) the words themselves do not have exactly the same meaning, or (b) the words do not have the same force, or (c) the associations and images are untranslatable, or (d) the style of saying them is different.

(3) Who says it:

Any language spoken during Eucharist should, in most cases, be spoken by a native speaker of the language. This is perhaps obvious. A problem arises however when there is a conflict between language fluency and ministerial appointment. Thus, for example, praying an intercessory prayer or singing a hymn is not usually a problem where these are commonly prayed or sung by members of the congregation. The homily or the eucharistic prayer, on the other hand, may and often does raise a problem on the grounds that these speech segments assume ministerial roles with prerequisite qualifications and there may not be a native speaker who has these qualifications.

The tendency in eucharistic communities is to provide training for ministry in the majority language(s) to the neglect of minorities. Two points need to be made here. First, the conflict between language fluency and ministerial appointment is acceptable only in the short term. In the long term, eucharistic communities can be said to have taken culture-inclusive language seriously only when they have provided training in liturgical competence for native speakers of minority languages so that the conflict no longer arises. Second, language inclusiveness in the Eucharist itself is a central part, but still only a part, of what is at stake here. The point of acquiring ministers with combined language fluency and ministerial appointment *within* Eucharist is that this establishes competence for other liturgical and service roles *outside of* the common Eucharist. Thus minority language groups are no longer always dependent upon ministers from the dominant language group.

We may note finally that all the difficulties arising from conflict between language fluency and ministerial appointment are exacerbated in the mono-presider. Few mono-presiders are fluent in more than two or three languages and many are fluent only in one. The result is that many mono-presiders either ignore entirely other languages besides their own or adopt the "worth-doing-badly" solution with mangled results. In Eucharists where the three-leader pattern rather than the mono-presider is adopted, the difficulties are considerably lessened. Still, whatever the current condition of liturgical leadership in a eucharistic community, the essential point here is that the coincidence of language fluency and ministerial appointment does not occur automatically but needs to be sought and planned for.

(4) How often languages are spoken:

I assume here that we are considering the regular Sunday Eucharist of a local community. The Eucharist does not need to be treated as all the same every time. Not every Eucharist has to be the same as those before and those after. And not every Eucharist needs to embody a solution to the issue of culture-inclusive language as if it were unrelated to any later or previous

Eucharists within the same community. Where there are many language groups in the community, culture-inclusive language needs to be sought rather in the long-term effect of the regular Eucharists of that community.

Not every significant language needs to be used in every Eucharist. A major consideration in culture-inclusive language is that of cohesiveness. A mix of many languages in one Eucharist can be chaotic. But when this same mix is spread out over several regular Sunday Eucharists over a period of time, the cohesiveness of each individual Eucharist liturgy can more easily be maintained.

(5) Where they are spoken:

One of the commonest solutions to multilingual local communities is that of "majority-rule." Minority language groups then establish their own regular Eucharists in their own language and separate from the local community. Hence, again the majority rules, but somewhere else and in a different language. There are pros and cons for this solution. On the positive side it does allow the various language groups of significant size to celebrate Eucharist in their own language. It does mean though some degree of failure in the *local* community, e.g. a local parish, because the character of a local community is precisely that it attempts to relate to and serve the local people *whatever their culture or needs*. A separate single-language Eucharist has been established in this case not because it is a Christian ideal, but because of a failure in the local community to provide for that language group. It is a kind of lesser of two evils solution, because the worse alternative would be total cultural domination, namely, that minority language groups would be required to worship God in a language foreign to them.

It is not a total failure because the catholicity of the church can still be recovered at a wider regional level. Thus, the various language groups may continue to encounter one another, but these become meetings *between* eucharistic communities rather than within a eucharistic community.

(6) Who decides:

The questions concerning which languages, what is said, who says it, how often, and where these languages are spoken, all depend in the end on who decides all this. Often these decisions are made by members of the dominant language group because they are already in charge and already make liturgical decisions. Those who are responsible for the liturgy decide quite rightly that their Eucharists should use culture-inclusive language. They then, with a little help from their other-language friends, set about doing just that. Thus decision-making for cultural inclusivity often excludes the culture it intends to include.

This is not quite so silly in practice, however, as it seems in cold ink. First, a demonstration of goodwill is required from the dominant language group. But the problem they face in many cases is that the minority language groups are either not used to being minority language groups (they are used to being a majority language group in some other place), or they are not used to participating actively in liturgy and do not themselves know how to go about it. After all, this is precisely the reality of the problem—if they were used to doing it, the Eucharist would already be culture-inclusive and there would be no problem.

Culture-inclusive language in Eucharist is achieved through negotiation over a long period of time. This does not ever quite come to a conclusion, because the political relationships between language groups, the relative sizes, and the transmission of language across generations are all in constant change. Whatever is agreed upon at one time needs to be negotiated again as circumstances change. There are two fundamental prerequisites however for successful negotiation: (a) In addition to and encouraged by the inclusiveness of Eucharist, there needs to be a continuous respectful interaction between the several language groups in a *non-liturgical* way. (b) Successful negotiation requires that from all language groups there are ministers and leaders who are competent both in the oratory of their own culture as well as in Christian liturgy. It is in terms of their *common liturgical competence* that the negotiations can be carried out among equals.

These prerequisites are not there, of course, at the beginning of
the search for culture-inclusive language. At the beginning we
must stumble along as best we can as long as this is seen to be
precisely a stumbling-along, a kind of pre-negotiation, attempting to put those prerequisites in place.

What Are the Theological Principles at Issue Here?

(1) *The catholicity of Eucharist.*

In the case of both gender-inclusive and culture-inclusive language one of the basic theological principles at stake is that of
the catholicity of Eucharist. Two aspects of this principle of
catholicity may need clarification here.

The first aspect is the concept of the *local* church. The essence
of a specifically *local* church is that it is composed, or at least is
intended to be composed, of any and all of the disciples of Christ
within that locality. It is the Eucharist as the regular and normal
gathering of that local church which is meant to express this
catholicity—a gathering of all, available to all. This is the sense in
which the Eucharist is (or is intended to be) both local and universal. It does not, or ought not to, discriminate among people
within a locality except on the basis of their intention to live as
disciples of Christ. This catholicity is expressed primarily in the
movements and gestures of communion—specifically the reception of the eucharistic bread and wine. What has been achieved
in the symbolism of movement and gesture at Communion,
serves as a model of what we are attempting to achieve in the
symbolism of speech through gender-inclusive and culture-
inclusive language.

In this respect, i.e., its catholicity in principle, the Eucharist of
a *local* church is different from a gender-based or language-
based or culture-based Eucharist which caters for men rather
than women or women rather than men, or a particular language group, or a particular culture, and makes no pretence to
cater for all and every Christian in a particular locality. In this
respect, too, a *local* church, and its Eucharist, is different from a

covenanted community where people meet for Eucharist because of some common bond or personal preference distinct from locality.

The church at large is made up of all these various communities and this variety of eucharistic assemblies. A Eucharist of a local church as, for example, a parish, precisely because it is local and not gender-based, nor language-based, nor otherwise gathered on some non-local basis, has a particular responsibility for the catholicity of the church. But such catholicity within the symbolism of Eucharist is notoriously difficult to achieve. There is a constant temptation to follow the discriminations that occur in society at large and replay them within the Eucharists of the local church. Hence, various other kinds of eucharistic assemblies become necessary to compensate for the lack of catholicity in the local church Eucharist.

Underlying, then, the attempts at gender- and culture-inclusive language in Eucharist is the striving to achieve a church catholic, i.e., a church which is both local and universal. The primary responsibility here lies on those communities which claim to be local. To the extent that the local communities are unable to achieve this within their own Eucharists, it becomes necessary to ensure that language-based or gender-based Eucharists are available so that overall the catholicity of the church is maintained.

The concept of the church catholic as both local and universal is a traditional one. A second aspect of catholicity to which we need to direct our attention is one that has come into prominence quite recently. This is the concept of *representation*. In the symbolism of Eucharist, some people "represent" others. The Eucharist does not take place in total silence and total stillness, nor does everyone speak all the time. Some persons speak or pray *for* others, or *to* others, or *on behalf* of others. A concern which has become prominent in modern times is the difficulty and delicacy with which one person may be entitled to represent other people from whom that person is significantly different. In brief, and in particular reference to the issue of gender- and culture-inclusive language, what is at issue here is the sense (or non-sense) in which a man may speak for both women and men and vice versa, and the sense in which a person of one culture may speak the language of or speak on behalf of people of another culture.

Historically this question did not receive much theological attention. It seems to have been assumed that goodwill and church legitimation were sufficient grounds for one person to represent others liturgically. Supporting this assumption was an accent on the common humanity of all people and a downplaying of cultural and gender diversity. A good deal of *mis*representation resulted from this assumption because the so-called "common humanity" has often turned out to be simply gender or cultural dominance by spokespersons who assumed that their culture or gender was everyone's humanity. In any case, we are now aware of needing to bring about the catholicity of the church in a way which our forebears were not, namely in its forms of representation. Thus a recently highlighted aspect of catholicity, for which our tradition is a liability rather than a resource, is that of representation. It is not just the language itself that is at issue, but *who* speaks it and *who* decides on behalf, that is as representative, of others.

(2) Criteria of inclusion and exclusion.

The catholicity of the church does not imply that anyone at all can be a member of the church regardless of their beliefs or behavior. Sometimes discussion on inclusiveness falters because it is assumed that the church should be completely inclusive, that it should not exclude anyone at all. But membership in the church cannot simply be "open to all" with no strings attached, and such an unprincipled open-door policy is not what is sought in the attempt to achieve gender- and culture-inclusive language in Eucharist. A totally open door would turn the church into a pointless, unprincipled organization with no standards, nor purpose, nor mission. The catholicity of the church means rather that people are included in or excluded from the church *on no other criteria* than those demanded by discipleship of Christ. No specific gender nor specific culture is required for Christian discipleship. Hence, when we do find gender or culture used as a criterion for exclusion from the Christian community, that exclusion is illegitimate and the principle of the catholicity of the church is thereby denied.

The criteria of inclusion and exclusion in the Christian community are attended to in a very deliberate and conscious way in the process and rites of initiation. Eucharist has a special role to play here, not only as the final rite of initiation into the Christian community, but also as the regular gathering of that community where inclusion and exclusion is played out in a more subtle and regular way. In principle, then, full participation in the church's Eucharist is open to everyone who is converted to Christ and sincerely tries to live out the Christian way of life. Some further refinements of this principle are possible, however, in the context of our current discussion:

(a) Criteria for inclusion and exclusion in Eucharist do not operate simply as all in or all out. There are *degrees* of participation in Eucharist. The criteria for inclusion at one degree of participation may be more restrictive than at another. We may distinguish three major degrees of participation in Eucharist. (i) Being present at the liturgy. At this degree of participation most contemporary churches adopt criteria which are quite inclusive. These may be summarized as an open-door policy except in cases of gross violations of hospitality such as loud interrupting noise, visually disruptive movements, drunkenness, offensive clothing or gestures. (ii) Receiving communion. At this degree of participation many churches adopt rather more exclusive criteria. These are likely to include explicit church membership and exclude grosser kinds of moral misbehavior outside Eucharist. (iii) Ministry within Eucharist. At this degree of participation most churches adopt criteria which are more exclusive again. These are likely to include clear formal membership in the church, Christian moral behavior outside Eucharist, and competence at that ministry.

(b) More subtle acts of inclusion and exclusion occur within Eucharist symbolism when some kinds of participants are treated as if they were not there or were someone else. This is a different kind of exclusion from that occurring in the degrees of participation discussed above. In this case it is not so much a physical and visible exclusion as a psychological and aural exclusion. This is the kind of exclusion we are normally dealing with when we confront the issue of gender-inclusive and culture-inclusive language. This is the case where both men and women participate in all three degrees of participation in Eucharist, but the language sounds as if only males were participant. This is the case also when people of a particular culture participate in Eucharist but their language never occurs there so that it is unimportant or peripheral or they participate as honorary members of another culture.

Thus the Christian community needs to be constantly alert that it does not profess one thing in its verbal theological statements but proclaim something else in the symbolism of its Eucharists. What is particularly alarming in the case of gender- and culture-exclusive liturgy is that time-honored tradition has been wrong here—frequently wrong in the case of culture-inclusive language and almost completely wrong in the case of gender-inclusive language. In these cases the traditional symbolism of Eucharist has been a source of error rather than a guide to genuine Christian practice and theology.

What Are the Practical Liturgical Effects?

I have addressed the issue of gender-inclusive language in terms of a participative process. What then are the practical steps which constitute a participative process of change to gender-inclusive God language?

The detailed ways of engaging in this process at a practical level will differ from community to community. The following list of proposed steps, provided it is used with flexibility, and allowing that the order of steps may need to alter in some communities, may be regarded as a gradated summary of this process of liturgical change. This list of steps has been chosen here in order to face two questions: (a) How to change to gender-inclusive God language without becoming bogged down in the issues of change as such, i.e., how to focus on God language while minimizing the irrelevant fear or excessive anger commonly aroused by liturgical change. (b) How to allow the community to control the speed of change and even to stop or reverse the process of change.

(1) Personally generated speech segments.

The homily, prayers created by the speaker, and various other personally generated speeches are commonly regarded as belonging to that speaker and are least likely to give offense when unaccustomed God language is introduced on the personal initiative of the speaker. These constitute a simple and acceptable way to introduce the community to new language and images of God. These are also the speech segments when speakers with old sexist habits need to exercise the greatest care that they do not slip back into sexist God language. God language is language both *to* God and *about* God. In either case this God language takes two main forms:

(a) *Nouns.* Commonly used nouns which inevitably connote a male, and mainly patriarchal, image of God are Lord, Father, King. A move toward gender-inclusive God language does not mean that such metaphors can never be used. It does mean, however, that their use needs to be greatly reduced and counterbalanced. Gender-inclusive nouns which are frequently used nowadays are such as Creator, Savior, Word, Nurturer, Sustainer, Source (of life, good, healing, etc.), and the word "God" itself without further imagining. Female images of God which can be used in combination with, or as a balance to, customary male images and still retain an overall gender-inclusive effect are Mother, Womb.

(b) *Qualifications.* The word "God" itself without further additions may often be used in language *about* God. In language *to* God, however, it is often too stark on its own and certainly so if it is used all the time. And if no other images of God are used people are left with their understanding of God filled in, so to speak, with the excessively male, and often patriarchal, images which they have inherited from liturgical tradition. These problems may be avoided by the use of "God" (and often other gender-inclusive nouns) with further qualification such as "Loving God," "God all compassionate," "Creator God," "God of peace," "Healing God."

(2) *Speech segments controlled by a written text.*

(a) Where words are controlled by a written text, the most acceptable changes are those made by the speaker who already has responsibility for that speech segment. Thus, for example, if the priest changes words in the eucharistic prayer to inclusive language this, in my experience, is usually acceptable to most of the congregation.
(b) In a similar way those with responsibility for the selection of texts, e.g., the selection of hymns or prayers of petition, may choose those with inclusive language.

(3) *Conflicts in responsibility for speech segments.*

Resistance to changing the words of a speech segment controlled by a written text may come from the speakers themselves who are reluctant to change the words of an authorized text.

(a) Changes to authorized contemporary texts by the responsible authority is the most satisfactory way of changing such text-dependent speech segments.
(b) There may be a considerable time lag between the realization that a change should be made and its actual production in newly produced liturgical texts. A particular community

may not responsibly want to wait that long. In that case some discussion and decision is required by the speakers of these texts on how to balance responsibility to the community with responsibility toward the currently authorized text.

(4) Biblical texts.

Scripture readings are more resistant to change than readings from contemporary authorized texts, and changing scripture readings raises different and more serious issues. Changing the scripture readings may take three forms:

(a) First, there is the issue of adequate translations. Part of the problem of sexist language is simply a problem of the translation of the original texts into sexist English. This problem can be solved by using modern gender-inclusive language translations. In most cases however this will involve gender-inclusive people language but not gender-inclusive God language.

(b) Once the issue of translation has been attended to, it is not normally the reader's responsibility to adapt the scripture readings to the contemporary community. This is a responsibility best left to the homilist and to the congregation as a whole. Part of the issue here is the manner in which the congregation listens to the scripture reading. Listening to a reading is a positive action on the part of the listener which takes place within a broader interpretative framework. Some congregations regard the scriptures as the word of God addressed to them in a very literal and immediate way. In this case the problem of sexist language seems to me to be insuperable. We may, however, regard our listening to the scripture readings as more in the mode of overhearing God speaking to a community of people in another time and place. This means we always make a cross-cultural interpretation from the culture-bound words of scripture in order to reach the word of God for us. We are already used to doing this for militaristic, violent, racist, aristocratic and unscientific words in scripture, and it is a relatively small step to add sexist words to the list. Moreover this "over-hearing" model reflects how Bible discussion or adequate commentary interprets scripture anyway. The culture-bound words of the scripture text do not suddenly become a direct address of God to us when they are read during liturgy. What I suggest here, then, in summary, is that the changing of sexist God language is not the responsibility of the liturgical reader, but rather that of the congregation as a whole and in particular of the homilist. If the congregation does not in fact listen to scripture in this interpretative way then this is an issue which needs to be addressed directly on its own as a congregational problem with much wider implications than just sexist God language.

(c) A third form of change of scripture that may be required is that of the selection of scripture texts read in Eucharist. The issue here is not so much the specific words within the text, but the selection of texts which present God in an overly mas-culine, and especially an overly patriarchal, way. The con-verse issue is that of the selection of texts which present only male responses to God. This issue of selection is one which needs to be addressed by planners of liturgy with an overall view of the entire cycle of Sunday readings.

(5) *Common formulae.*

Changing the baptismal formula, Our Father, trinitarian blessings and conclusions again raises an issue of change differ-ent in kind from those discussed above. This is the area of most contention. We are in an age when the theological disputes and need for a culturally relevant reformulation of Christian faith which produced the traditional credal formulations are no longer ours. We must engage now with quite new requirements and produce correspondingly appropriate formulations of basic belief. This process is under way and it is not carried out inde-pendently of liturgy. I do not think there is as yet any sure path to be followed here. It is still not yet clear what substitutes for the traditional "Father, Son, and Holy Spirit" formulation are appropriate. We will need to attempt new formulations but with a certain tentativeness rather than belligerence. Two factors in particular contribute to this tentativeness:

(a) At a strict theological level of adequate expression of Christian trinitarian belief, new formulations tend each to have their own inadequacies so that they are often no better than the traditional formulation. Hence, no new formulation can as yet make strong claims to be the successor to the "Father, Son, and Holy Spirit" formula for specifically liturgical usage.

(b) The trinitarian formulae are ones for which communities seldom confer responsibility on particular ministers or planners. Hence, changes here need to proceed at the pace and rhythm of that community's own reformulation of its faith. In other words, trinitarian reformulations cannot be treated as an issue of change with a clearly desirable goal, but rather as a community's tentative groping where the goal itself is not yet clear. Some of the trinitarian formulae which are now used or proposed for use in liturgy include: God, Son, and Spirit; Creator, Redeemer, Sanctifier; Creator, Brother, Friend; Parent, Brother/Sister, Advocate; Mother, Lover, Friend; Source of all being, Eternal Word, Holy Spirit.

(6) Feedback.

Perhaps the most important factor of all in change is feedback from members of the congregation. There will nearly always be resistance to change as such from within a congregation, i.e., resistance to any change at all irrespective of the intrinsic merits of the old or the new language. Some negative criticism of any change can always therefore be expected. Negative criticism is usually more vocal than positive approval. Positive feedback from among the participants to speakers who use inclusive God language reduces the isolation of those who attempt change.

In the case of *culture*-inclusive language, it is not so easy to list a sequence of practical steps in liturgical change because the starting points of intercultural relationships may differ greatly from one eucharistic community to another. What is possible here is to list the main principles which should guide a change to more culture-inclusive language at Eucharist.

(1) Culture-inclusive language in the Eucharist of a local church needs to be treated as an overall plan within a large time frame, e.g., over a period of a year. Here successful culture-inclusive language differs from gender-inclusive language. Gender-inclusive language is an issue within *every* Eucharist. Culture-inclusive language refers to an overall effect *over a period of time*.

(2) Culture-inclusive language in Eucharist requires

(a) the inclusion of the significant languages of the local community within the local community Eucharists;
(b) coordination of these local Eucharists with special language Eucharists where these are needed;
(c) the elimination within any one language spoken at Eucharist of false assumptions about other language groups.

(3) Culture-inclusive language in Eucharist requires a decision not just about the inclusion of significant languages but also a decision about which speech segments can most appropriately be spoken in one language rather than another.

(4) Speech segments in any language should be spoken by native speakers of that language. A community has achieved culture-inclusive language when it has sufficient ministers so that ministerial appointment and language fluency are not in conflict.

(5) Planning for culture-inclusive language and the means to achieve it needs to include representatives of the language groups concerned.

Beyond Liturgy

In the changes to both gender-inclusive and culture-inclusive language, one of the key features is community participation in these changes. This is a key feature because the aim of liturgical change is not just the Eucharist liturgy itself but changes in the post-liturgical lives of the participants.

In the case of gender-inclusive language, the key feature is not individual change to gender-inclusive God language, but an engagement of the whole community in reexamining and changing their shared images and understanding of God, and thereby also their own gender stereotypes and gender relationships.

In the case of culture-inclusive language, the key feature is an engagement of several language groups to achieve a genuinely bicultural or multicultural community in all its aspects.

Chapter 3

The Relevance of Liturgical Language

The Issue

I use the word "relevance" here to indicate a quality of language whereby (a) the words are *lucid* to the majority of the congregation (the participants know what the words mean), (b) the words *belong* to that community (they carry a sense that they are "ours"), and (c) the words are *life-giving* (it is worth paying attention to these words because they carry life and hope). Language becomes a problem, and its relevance an issue, when we no longer expect these words to change us or engage the rest of our lives.

As in the previous chapter, the issue discussed here is restricted to speech and does not deal with other kinds of symbolic systems even though these others (gesture, posture, furniture, movement, etc.) may also be said to constitute a "language." The issue raised here overlaps to some extent with the issue of inclusiveness discussed in the previous chapter since questions of inclusiveness are in many aspects questions also of relevance. Exclusive language such as sexist language may be considered an extreme form of irrelevance. But even when liturgical language is gender- and culture-inclusive, the issue of its relevance may remain. Irrelevance is not so extreme as exclusion, or perhaps it is just a slower form of it. It is a dulling of attention, a reduction of communication, or the takeover of liturgy by a dominant elite.

There is some tendency among English-speakers (not always the case for other languages) to take it for granted that words have lost their power to change our lives. So many of the spoken words in our lives are lies, trivialities, banalities and advertisements. And the English-speaking liturgy makes its own contribution to all of these. If we have lost faith in the power of words and oratory in general, why should oratory to God be any different!

The issue of relevance arises when our prayers in particular and our liturgical language in general contain a lot of words or phrases which do not say very much, do not engage us much. It arises when a good deal of our liturgical language is no longer lucid, does not seem to belong to us, or has ceased to be life-giving.

The eucharistic prayer is one of the important speech segments of Eucharist and it may serve to illustrate what we are attempting to grapple with here. In recent liturgical research, liturgists have given a great deal of attention to the *origins* and *history* of the eucharistic prayer. Historical versions of this prayer have become treasuries of theological ideas, storehouses of traditional wisdom, criteria of truth and orthodoxy.

For many regular participants in Eucharist, however, the eucharistic prayer is taken rather as an occasion for private meditation. This means that the eucharistic prayer becomes a holy time set aside for God when we may pursue our own private and preferably God-directed thoughts while someone else prays necessary but dull prayers. Important things are going on while these prayers are being said, but the *words* of the prayers do not require attention. They need not engage us. We do not expect to hear life-giving, life-changing words in them. In such a case the liturgical language has lost relevance. This is the issue which occupies us in this chapter. Thus our focus and concern here is not so much to do with liturgical prayers as treasuries of theological ideas, storehouses of traditional wisdom, or criteria of truth and orthodoxy. These are indeed legitimate concerns. But they are not our point of focus here. What concerns us here is whether our current prayers are lucid, ours, and life-giving. What is at issue here is their *relevance*.

Consider the following examples of the openings words of some modern eucharistic prayers:

(1) From the Roman Rite: Eucharistic Prayer II:
"Father, it is our duty and our salvation, always and everywhere to give you thanks through your beloved Son, Jesus Christ."[1]

(2) From the Anglican New Zealand Prayer Book: Eucharistic Liturgy:
"It is right indeed, it is our joy and our salvation, holy Lord, almighty Father, everlasting God, at all times and in all places to give you thanks and praise through Christ your only Son."[2]

(3) From the Roman Rite: Eucharistic Prayers (B: Jesus Our Way):
"We thank you, strong and holy God. In wisdom you guide the course of the world and cherish all of us with tender care."[3]

These illustrations though brief serve here to indicate that we may approach and relate to God in rather different ways. More importantly for our purposes here, however, they further illustrate the initial impact of liturgical words in conveying impressions such as "something interesting is going on here," or "I've heard all this before," or "this is worth paying attention to and getting involved in," or "these words are beyond me," etc. In the congregations with which I am familiar, the triteness and foreignness of the language in example (1) and (2) would convey to the congregation that no attention need be given to the rest of this prayer.

The examples I have used here are only partial illustrations of the issue and suffer from some serious limitations which we need to recognize. The first limitation is that I have used examples here from *written* liturgical texts. This is necessary here because I am engaged in a similarly written explanation. But

---

[1] *The Roman Missal* (Sydney: E.J. Dwyer, 1969) p. 493.

[2] *A New Zealand Prayer Book: He Karakia Mihinare o Aotearoa* (Auckland: William Collins Publishers, 1989) p. 421.

[3] *Eucharistic Prayers (A. God Guides the Church; B. Jesus Our Way; C. Jesus, Model of Love; D. The Church on the Road to Unity)* (International Committee on English in the Liturgy, 1989).

liturgies are not made up of *written* texts. Even if they are dependent on written texts, liturgical speech segments are *spoken*. The relevance of liturgical language is primarily an issue of spoken words. Written texts are only one of several contributors to an actual liturgical speech segment. My illustrations are limited secondly because irrelevance is not usually a matter of one or two sentences, but is rather an accumulation of words or a prolonged manner of speaking.

The point at which a congregation, or part of it, has decided that the liturgical language is irrelevant is usually fairly easy to detect. When a congregation has "turned off," we can usually detect it in their body language—especially their facial expressions and posture. Sometimes this occurs during the course of a speech segment as irrelevant language accumulates. Sometimes it occurs right at the outset as the congregation has learned from past experience that nothing life-giving need be expected there. While irrelevance itself is usually clearly signalled by the congregation, its causes are more complex and likely to be a combination of several factors. The major factors may usefully be listed as follows:

(1) The speaker: The speakers themselves (whether homilist, reader, person who prays a particular prayer, commentator, announcer) already convey associations and social indicators which may contribute to irrelevance even apart from their manner of speaking or the content of their speech. For example, a particular speaker has spoken too much or too dully before, is not in touch with some or all of the congregation in terms of age group, culture, political leanings, attitudes to people, type and range of vocabulary. Thus a middle-aged speaker may already suggest dullness to a teenager, while a teenage speaker immediately attracts attention. A simple change of speaker from one speech segment to another may attract attention, while the same speaker speaking yet again invites inattention.

(2) The manner of speaking: As contributing to irrelevance the manner of speaking needs to be considered on three levels corresponding to the three elements of relevance:

(a) From the aspect of "lucidity," speech which is inaudible, over-amplified, not clearly enunciated contributes to irrelevance.

(b) From the aspect of "belonging," the speaker's accent, choice of vocabulary, and style of phrasing are likely to identify the speaker with, or distance the speaker from, all or some of the congregation.

(c) From the aspect of being "life-giving," speech may on the one hand lack conviction indicating that the speaker does not really believe these words or on the other hand it may be overladen with such personal intensity that the words sound insincere. The kind of conviction required will differ according to the nature of the speech segment. A person who prays a personally created prayer needs to do so with the conviction of something to which they are personally committed and in their own personal words. A reader of scripture, on the other hand, cannot read scripture as if these were personally created words full of personal commitment, i.e., a reader is not meant to act the part of the original writer. Nevertheless, there is a very big difference between the reader who simply reads clearly and the reader who conveys to the listeners the conviction that there is something important going on here. Most difficult of all are representative prayers, i.e., prayers controlled by a written text which someone prays on behalf of the whole congregation, such as collect prayers or eucharistic prayers in the Roman and Anglican traditions. These prayers require conviction but not idiosyncrasy on the part of the speaker. The speaker who does not believe that the words of the prayer are important and life-giving almost inevitably destroys the prayer's relevance to the congregation. But the speaker who makes such prayers sound as if they were being personally generated on the spot from internal conviction reduces them to silliness.

(3) The content of speech: Irrelevance in words and phrases is dependent upon culture, and can vary from one generation to another, or even one decade to another, within the same language. Most important are the words which convey our images of God and the ways in which we relate to God or God to us. Constant repetitions of "Father" and "Lord" in reference to God turn a major element of prayer, the way we address God, into clichés. If the images of God are narrow and predictable, then we learn to expect no life there. In addition to the images of God, the more general style and vocabulary of our liturgical language can cause irrelevance. In the congregations with which I am familiar the following expressions are likely contributors to irrelevance:

(a) Traditional phrases almost unintelligible to the ear untrained in traditional theology: "our paschal sacrifice," "salvation," "righteousness."

(b) Phrases which impose upon us sentiments that are embarrassing or seem like grovelling or are simply unlikely: "He came to take away sin, which keeps us from being friends, and hate, which makes us all unhappy." (Roman Missal: Eucharistic Prayer for Children II); "Thank you for counting us worthy to stand in your presence and serve you" (Roman Missal: Eucharistic Prayer II); "Now we watch for the day, hoping that the salvation promised us will be ours when Christ our Lord will come again in his glory" (Roman Missal: Advent Preface I).

A Way Forward

Some elements of a solution are more obvious than others and often simple to implement. Let me list these first before we turn to the more complex elements.

(1) Read words and said words.

One element in the solution is a change in the relative proportions of "read" words and "said" words. This distinction is not concerned with the *content* of the words but with the *manner* in which they are spoken. "Read" words are those where the speaker pays close attention to a written text, i.e., the speaker's eyes are concentrated mainly on a book. The focus is on seeing rather than hearing. "Said" words are those where the speaker pays close attention to the sound rather than the sight of the words, i.e., the speaker listens rather than looks. The focus in this case is on hearing rather than seeing. Both read words and said words are a normal part of liturgy. In the case of *read* words, however, the speaker is focusing away from the congregation, i.e., toward a book. In the case of *said* words the speaker is engaged in the same activity as the congregation, namely, listening.

An *excess* of read words contributes to irrelevance since it disengages the speaker from the congregation. Thus an excess of read words is a strategy of the wooden-puppet type of liturgical leader who disengages from the congregation and engages in a reading of texts, an essentially private activity done aloud so that others may overhear but not intrude.

This is not to imply, however, that *said* words are always better. An *excess* of said words is the strategy of demagogues and egotists delighted by the sound of their own voices. This is another issue not so much about the relevance of language as about the use of language for personal power or self-aggrandizement. This need not concern us just here except to note that an excess of said words carries its own though different liabilities.

The liturgical value of *read* words when not excessive is that they turn attention to the community's sacred texts, its scriptures, its communal prayer traditions. Read words allow the congregation to pay more attention to the written words and less to the speaker's idiosyncratic interpretation of them. It is the *excess* of read words that contributes to irrelevance. Long periods of read words easily become dull and lifeless. Few preachers today would attempt a read sermon, though this seems to have been possible in the past. For most congregations with a book-based liturgical tradition the attempt to increase the relevance of their liturgical language will involve a moderate shift from read to said words in their scripture readings, and a large shift from read to said words in their major prayers. For congregations with a tradition emphasizing spontaneous prayer, the problem is more likely to be one of fashionable triteness or simply oratorical inadequacy. It is likely to require a shift in the opposite direction, i.e., toward more read words.

(2) Spontaneous and prepared prayer.

A second and again relatively simple element in the solution is the recognition of the distinction between spontaneous prayer and prepared prayer. There are cultural differences here. An individualistic culture is likely to regard the *inner person* as the location of truth and sincerity and to treat conformity with some suspicion. A more corporate or socially conscious culture is likely to regard *common accord* as the location of truth and loyalty and regard individual idiosyncrasy with suspicion. In the first case spontaneous prayer which comes from the heart will be valued. In the second case prepared (whether memorized or written) prayers which have been socially sanctioned will be valued. Both of these tendencies are contained within European church traditions. The point of recognition which concerns us here is that both these prayer styles can contribute to either the relevance or the irrelevance of language but the contribution of each is different.

Spontaneous prayer contributes to *ir*relevance when it follows set formulae memorized and unconsciously reproduced within a particular prayer tradition, and when the speaker's capacity as wordsmith is simply unequal to the task. It contributes to the relevance of prayer on the other hand by its freshness, its originality and its direct connection with the immediate life situations of these particular participants. *Prepared* prayer contributes to *ir*relevance when it remains within set formulae developed in other times and places. It contributes to relevance on the other hand when the time, care, and talent given to its composition give life, variety, simplicity and beauty to the prayer.

(3) Translations.

A further element of a way forward centers on the problem of *translations*. A great number of prepared prayers in current usage in the Roman rite are translations. The use of translations of prayers is perhaps the greatest of all contributors to the irrelevance of liturgical language. Translations of prayers can sometimes be successful. Sometimes the translated languages and images can be startling and challenging to the recipient culture. For the most part, however, translated prayers rarely resonate with the religious sentiments, images and theology of another culture. When publicly proclaimed rather than simply read privately, they frequently violate the rhythms and cadences of the recipient language, especially its oratorical styles. The foreignness of such language sends a convincing message to the congregation that nothing serious nor life-engaging can be expected to occur here. It affects the speakers more perhaps than the listeners as they make their way through these awkward phrases in compassionate haste, in a stilted sing-song, or in embarrassing sincerity. And speaker after speaker of prayer translations from foreign languages into English, convinces the congregation Sunday after Sunday that whatever is going on here it need not be taken too seriously. A major element in the solution to irrelevant language is the avoidance of all translations except where there is some compelling and particular reason for regarding a particular translation as an exception to the rule.

So far I have been concerned with the simpler elements in a solution, namely those concerned with the style of speaking, the origins of the words, and the issue of translation. The more difficult issue centres however around the *content* of the speaking— the selection of words and their combinations.

I do not want to suggest that there is simple solution here. The solution consists in discovering or producing good literature (for reading aloud), good (spoken) poetry, good oratory, good rhetoric. There are no very clear rules for this that I am aware of. There are some clues, however, within recent liturgical experience. These clues lie within those parts of the liturgy in which we have indeed experimented for some time, namely, the language of *hymns* and *homilies*. The amount of time and care given to hymns and homilies, and the sheer number of people working hard at these two kinds of speech segments, give us some indication of the size of the solution required if we seek relevance for the whole of our liturgical language.

The language of hymns is one part of liturgical language which has not rested simply upon spontaneity nor been content with the language of past times and other cultures. The language of hymns illustrates, too, how words can be life-giving, powerful, influential. At the same time it illustrates the difficulty of achieving such relevance in language. For every life-giving relevant hymn there must be dozens, perhaps hundreds, that are silly, banal, sentimentalized, or theologically bad. On top of that, hymns may be relevant to some people but not to others. The experiments, adventures and misadventures in the language of hymns gives us more than a clue and rather an indication of the size of the undertaking, with its never-ending character.

The language of homilies gives us further clues to this undertaking. Hymns are most commonly designed for common congregational participation. Homilies are more to do with the interaction of an individual (the homilist) with the congregation. Homilies thus give more scope for individuality and inventiveness. Again though, our experience with homilies gives an indication of the size and dimensions of the question of relevance in liturgical language. Homilies range from boring, upsetting, misleading, or idiotic to humorous, insightful, truthful, life-engaging. They may be about real human lives or they may be abstract repetitions of tired words.

Hymns and homilies are two examples of liturgical speech segments where the issue of relevance has been engaged for some time. They may provide us with at least partial models of the size and dimensions of the enterprise of achieving relevance in the whole of our liturgical language. Certainly they indicate that relevance in liturgical language is something for which we will need to search together for a long time yet.

What Are the Theological Principles at Issue Here?

The theological impetus to engage in a search for relevant liturgical language is dependent upon: (1) Our strategies concerning the relationship between church and society, (2) The importance we attach to the effectiveness of liturgy, (3) The relative emphasis we place on individual or community.

(1) The relationship between church and society.

The issue of relevant liturgical language is part of the more general issue of the relevance of the church to the society of which it is part. There are several different scenarios possible here. For our purposes we may simplify these by reducing them to two.

If the church is concerned with setting up barriers against an intrusive society, then it is consistent to set up processes of socialization into the church which are alternative to those of the society. An integral part of such processes would be the development and transmission of a specialized church language, i.e., a countercultural or politically resistant language. This amounts to a deliberate option for irrelevance in liturgical language. The church and its liturgy are deliberately setting up an alternative system of beliefs and rituals, and people are presented with a clear option for it or against it. If they opt for the church, they will then be initiated into its specialized liturgical language. And this will distinguish them clearly from the ways of the world.

The point to notice here, for it is often overlooked by proponents of relevance, is that the *ir*relevance of liturgical language should not be judged obviously and always bad. It may be a strategic decision within the broader political stance of the church. Thus, a liturgical language which is to some degree irrelevant to the wider society may be a language of resistance for a church under persecution or under threat from dominating forces in society. Within this broader strategy, the irrelevance of liturgical language is consistent and unproblematic. It is a defensive measure, a logical and consistent element of a more general strategy of the church to separate itself (or maintain a separation) from the dominant power structures and corrupting ideologies of an intrusive society.

The irrelevance of liturgical language becomes problematic, and in that sense an issue needing a solution, when we have already made an option for closer communication between church and society. Or put another way, it becomes problematic when we expect consistency between our liturgical language and our everyday non-liturgical language. In this case, we want a liturgical language which allows ease of access between church and society. This ease of access has a double intention. (a) It intends that the liturgy itself be lucid to non-church members who on various occasions and for various reasons attend Christian liturgies. (b) Perhaps more importantly, it intends also that for church members themselves the liturgical language is easily transferred to non-liturgical situations. Thus, the liturgical language provides church members with a vocabulary and articulation of their beliefs which can communicate quite immediately to the wider society where they spend most of their lives. Rather than developing processes of socialization into church language, attention is given here to using as far as is appropriate the language of society in the church's liturgy.

Although the theological issues in the relationship between church and society are rather more complicated than I am able to describe here, the options outlined above serve to indicate that an engagement in the search for relevant liturgical language rests on a previous theological-political stance.

(2) *Liturgical effectiveness.*

The relevance of liturgical language reaches the status of a priority issue in the symbolism of Eucharist only if we place high value on liturgical *effectiveness*. Liturgical "effectiveness" here refers to the changes for the better which occur in people's lives as a result of their participation in a liturgy. "Better" is here understood as a more authentic commitment to being disciples of Christ. Thus, very simply, liturgy is effective if the participants' post-liturgical lives are more Christian than they were beforehand.

Effectiveness, however, is not the only criterion by which spoken words in fact become part of liturgy. Two other criteria often used are the *orthodoxy* of the words and the liturgical *tradition* of words. Often these two are intermingled, or confused. Traditional liturgical words may be seen to be orthodox, and may come to be the only clearly orthodox words, i.e., *new* words appear to be *un*orthodox. Or alternatively, words clearly known to be theologically orthodox are, for that very reason, brought into liturgy and may come to eliminate or forbid other liturgically viable words.

Orthodoxy or tradition (or both) are often given greater weight than effectiveness in the preparation of liturgical speeches and texts. The *relevance* of liturgical language becomes important only if we place a high value on liturgical *effectiveness* (as defined above), rather than just on liturgical orthodoxy or tradition.

We may note here that international liturgical texts prepared for a large variety of congregations, i.e., not tailored to quite particular congregations, have difficulty coping with the very concrete level at which liturgies are effective (or ineffective) in people's lives. Even relatively minor changes in language and life-style from region to region, from urban to rural, from migrant to native-born, may affect the relevance of liturgical language. There is no such thing as effectiveness "in general." A Eucharist is a particular complex of actions in which particular nameable people participate and which have particular post-liturgical effects in the lives of those people. Liturgical texts, unless they are prepared for particular known congregations, cannot cope with this level of concreteness.

Thus a priority concern with relevant liturgical language rests upon the relative value we place upon orthodoxy, tradition or effectiveness as criteria for appropriate liturgical language. There need not, and should not, be any conflict here in the abstract. At the level of actual liturgical speech, however, that is, at the level of actual choices between the liturgical use of some particular words rather than others, there often is a conflict between orthodoxy/tradition on the one hand and effectiveness on the other.

This question needs some further investigation here for often it is not so much the value placed on liturgical effectiveness as such that is under debate but rather the *manner of achieving* this effectiveness. Again here for the sake of simplicity let me propose the issue in the form of an option between two basic positions.

There is a view of liturgical effectiveness which emphasizes the importance of *the right actions being done and the right words being said*. In this view it is good but not vital that the recipients of the liturgical action actually comprehend the words that are said. A distinction between a "sacramental action" (including the words), which must be performed by a competent minister in order to be valid, and "ecclesiastical rites," which are words and actions not strictly necessary but which add clarity and richness to the liturgy, is coherent with this view. In this view only the strictly sacramental words (words of consecration or of invocation of the Spirit) are strictly necessary for effectiveness. All the other words are much less important, icing on the cake at best. In the clearest case of this position, the liturgy may be said in an archaic language barely understood by the congregation. This is the extreme case of the view that the effectiveness of the liturgy is dependent mainly upon the words of the liturgical ministers, and minimally on the relevance of the liturgical speech to the congregation. In a less extreme version, there are many liturgical leaders for whom only the language of the homily needs to be strictly relevant to the congregation; most of the rest of the liturgy is the "church's" language and need not be relevant to the congregation as long as they know in a broad sense what is going on. According to this view, the liturgy is fundamentally the action of God—it is mystery. Relevance is important in the homily, but not in the rest of the liturgical action where mystery is more important than relevance.

In contrast to the above, there is another view of liturgical effectiveness which sees the whole of the liturgical action, including the totality of its spoken words, as contributing toward the effects of that liturgy. In this case, a major contribution to the effectiveness of liturgy is precisely the comprehension and appropriation by the congregation of the spoken words. Here the relevance of the spoken words becomes a major consideration in the preparation and performance of liturgy. This is the position which underpins and gives impetus to a priority consideration for the relevance of liturgical speech.

(3) Emphasis on individual or community.

A third theological principle underlying considerations of relevance in liturgical language is that of the relative importance attached to the individual or to the community in Christian faith and practice. The principle which the above proposals for relevant liturgical language seek to apply is that there should be a balance so that the individual person is not treated as if separate from community, nor is the community allowed to eradicate the uniqueness of the individual person.

Let me again here illustrate this principle by collapsing it into its extremes. An extreme emphasis on *community* would emphasize uniformity of language even to the use of a liturgical language which is comprehensible to no one in the congregation. An extreme emphasis on the *individual* would emphasize spontaneous speech expressing sentiments from within the interior of the individual even if this results in a speaking "in tongues" which no one else can understand. The two extremes ironically both lead to incomprehensibility even though one does so in the interests of external mystery and the other in the interests of internal feeling.

A liturgical emphasis on one side or the other rests upon a theological position holding either that divine communication occurs in some primary way within the structure of the church or on the other hand that it occurs within the interiority of the individual person. In more traditional terms, this difference appears as a theological emphasis either on *community* faith (the faith of the church) or on *personal* faith (the faith of the individual). An emphasis on the faith of the church will tend to value prayer said in common since such prayer derives from the church itself as the primary location of divine communication. An emphasis on personal faith will tend to value spontaneous prayer since such prayer derives from the interiority of the individual person as the primary location of divine communication.

No serious modern theology could treat community faith and personal faith as in competition. Theological considerations require the constant interweaving, the maintaining of a continuous interaction, between personal faith and the faith of the church, between individual and community. These theological considerations suggest that liturgical language similarly needs to reflect this constant interweaving within liturgy of communal and individual contributions. Thus set formulae of prayer which are prayed in common or by a representative should contribute both to the building up of the community and to the personal life of the individuals within it. But spontaneous and personally formulated prayers of individuals within the liturgy should also contribute both to the building up of the community and to the individuals within it.

What Are the Practical Liturgical Effects?

(1) Oratorical skills.

A search for relevance in liturgical language will pay careful attention to the oratorical traditions and practices of the society. Two things are implied here when we pay attention to oratory:

(a) We need to draw upon the words and speech patterns of the local culture (i) rather than on translations from other languages, (ii) rather than on English in general or written English or the dominant forms of English without regard to its dialects and local variations, and (iii) rather than on a local tradition of peculiarly church language.
(b) We distinguish between oratory and other styles of speech.

For spontaneous and personally generated prayers people will usually use their normal spoken language, with a tendency toward its more formal style. It is the frankness of "normal" speech, though not slang, that is required for these kinds of prayers. For the more formal and representative prayers, spoken by the congregation in common or by a minister on behalf of the congregation, there is a different requirement. This requirement is the skills and power of oratorical language, that is, of more self-consciously sculptured, more deliberately attractive and persuasive language.

(2) *Liturgical competence.*

"Competence" has two senses in application to liturgy. In a legal or organizational sense it refers to a minister's right and duty to play a particular role in liturgy. Or put conversely, some liturgical roles can be performed legitimately only by a person appointed to that ministry. This official appointment confers on that person the competence to perform that ministry. In a second sense, "competence" refers to the performative skills of a person to perform *well* a particular liturgical task. In the first sense, then, it refers to a person's official appointment to perform a liturgical role. In the second sense it refers to a person's proficiency in performing a liturgical role.

It is in this second sense of "competence" that attention to the relevance of liturgical language will require practical liturgical change for many, perhaps most, liturgical speakers. Competence in this sense does not imply total spontaneity in liturgical speeches for this relies too much on the instantaneous and idiosyncratic language power of the speaker. Nor on the other hand does it imply total reliance on carefully crafted written or remembered speeches. It requires an ability of the minister responsible for a particular speech segment to be able to use and alter prepared texts in ways relevant to the congregation yet without imposing on them the minister's own idiosyncrasies.

(3) *A variety of voices.*

The relevance of liturgical language is not merely about using relevant words. It is essentially about *spoken* words. Beautifully relevant phrases spoken by a boring voice, or by the same voice all the time, become liturgically irrelevant even if they look good on paper. A variety of speakers of speech segments, and thus a variety of voices, personalities, and representations, is an important contributor to relevance in liturgical language.

(4) *Attention to the function of each speech segment.*

Liturgical relevance further requires careful attention to the function of each speech segment. This is a consequence of the requirements of oratorical skill, liturgical competence, and variety. Relevance is defeated by an overall sameness in speeches or by speech styles inappropriate to the nature of a particular speech segment. Thus:

(a) *Communal speech segments:* hymns, repetitive responses, traditional recitations (creeds, the Lords Prayer). These are characterized by their being spoken by many people together. They are therefore dependent upon standard texts whether read or memorized. They do not permit individual creativity at the time of speaking.

(b) *Community intercessions.* These are intercessions for immediate needs. They require freshness, frankness and a directness that comes from the desire for help. This is most easily achieved in individually created prayers. If they are said by representatives on behalf of the congregation, this directness needs to remain. Once their language attains a formality similar to that of more formal ministerial prayers (such as a eucharistic prayer or a collect) they lose their specific relevance and drop back into a general sameness.

(c) *Invitations and directions.* These are usually short speech segments and require a graciousness of language which is neither peremptory nor excessively elaborate.

(d) *Homily.* This speech segment permits the most individually crafted language. This is the speech segment over which the individual speaker exercises most control, and in this sense it needs to be seen as complementary to the scripture readings where the speaker is most constrained by the written text.

(e) *Scripture readings.* These are speech segments over which the individual speaker and indeed the community exercises least control. On the contrary, these speech segments serve as measures of the community's faithfulness. They can afford to have the least contemporary relevance of liturgical speeches since their function is to measure authenticity rather than relevance. Their relevance, however, may be affected at two levels: First, they need to be read clearly so that their meaning can be grasped at one hearing (lucid). Second, they need to be read with conviction that here is a message vital to this community (life-giving).

(f) *Eucharistic prayers.* These are dialogue prayers where an individual speaker and the congregation combine in a prayer which expresses the congregation's most essential and unifying relationship to God in thanksgiving and intercession. The communal segments are controlled by communal texts. The individual segments permit only slight individual creativity since these are representative prayers on behalf of the whole congregation. Their relevance is measured by their ability to express in contemporary form the community's memory and hope.

(g) *Shorter ministerial prayers:* collect-type prayers, blessings, intercessions. These permit some individual creativity, but their function is not to express the personal spirituality of the speaker but rather to articulate the community's hope in very brief form and usually in relation to a particular theme or a particular stage of the liturgy.

(5) *Gathering and sending.*

We need to pay particular attention to the gathering and sending rites of Eucharist since these particular rites have the specific function of articulating very concisely the relevance of the Eucharist to the world from which the participants have come and the world into which the participants will return. Thus the gathering rite (hymn, welcome, collect prayer, and perhaps other penitential or praise-giving prayers or silence) has the function of shifting the congregation from its prior activities and concerns into a liturgical assembly. This normally requires some amount of time, some formality, some communal activity or speech, a focusing of attention on the specific identity and purpose of this assembly. The sending rite, on the other hand, serves to focus and articulate what has been happening within that assembly in a way which does not allow it to rest content with itself but moves it outward toward the world beyond liturgy. Thus a kind of generalized relevance of language is not specific enough for the rites of gathering and sending. What is required for them is that specific relevance which clearly focuses on each of these quite different directions of either gathering in or sending out.

(6) *The creation of texts.*

A move toward more relevant liturgical language depends upon (a) an increase in the competence of the speakers of liturgical speech segments, and (b) the creation of relevant texts for those speech segments which are text-dependent. A good deal of work has already been done on modern written texts. But, (a) many liturgical speakers still rely upon English translations of original Latin or Greek texts and this involves the speaker in a constant battle with the irrelevance of the text, (b) no English text is adequate for all dialects of English and speakers still need to adapt the written text in a way relevant to their own congregations, (c) the greater the irrelevance of the text, the greater the danger of speakers ignoring them and indulging inappropriately their own idiosyncrasies and personal spiritualities, i.e., turning representative prayers into personal prayers. The creation of relevant liturgical texts thus becomes a major item in the search for relevant liturgical language.

Beyond Liturgy

The driving force of the search for relevant liturgical language lies particularly in the consideration of its effects beyond the space and time of the liturgical action itself. Relevant language is directly to do with the transfer between the Eucharist and daily non-liturgical life. Irrelevant language conceals the manner in which daily life should be transformed in Eucharist and the impact Eucharist should have on daily life. Irrelevant language thus contributes to the contradictions between what is said in Eucharist and our behavior outside Eucharist.

The purpose of the search for relevant liturgical language is that participants in a Eucharist encounter there an articulation of Christian faith which immediately confirms, challenges or transforms the goals and values which directed their lives before they entered that Eucharist. Participants then leave that Eucharist with a new or renewed articulation of the Christian message for their daily lives. If this can be achieved, the amount of translation required to understand what daily life means to Eucharist or Eucharist means to daily life is minimized. Continuous doses of irrelevant liturgical language on the other hand maximize the gap between Eucharist and our daily interpretation of life's tasks and meaning.

Chapter 4

The Inculturation of Symbols and Calendar

The Issue

In the last two chapters I was concerned with language as speech. But as well as spoken language there are many other symbolic systems, and in that sense "languages," by which liturgical communication takes place. There are a number of issues here relating to such symbolic systems as posture (e.g., standing, sitting, kneeling), gesture (e.g., of welcome, dismissal, enclosure, emphasis), movement (e.g., approach and withdrawal, processions, where ministers come from and go to), arrangement of space (e.g., issues of facing, where the main foci should be, issues of sanctuary and foyer), dress (e.g., use of traditional local costumes, archaic dress, everyday contemporary clothing). There is also a whole set of issues to do with the liturgically appropriate use of cultural items not previously used in liturgy. One or several of such issues is likely to become a focus of concern for most communities at some time or another. In many communities such issues often also become intricately entangled with people's stances for or against change as such. However, in most of these areas some kind of inculturation is already taking place. It may be too fast or too slow. Sometimes it is judged as success and sometimes as failure. But it is happening and it is not difficult to point to examples of such inculturation.

The more difficult area of inculturation, and the one on which I want to focus here as a key issue, along with the issues of leadership and speech already discussed, centers around the liturgical calendar. At its core, this issue concerns the relationship within Christianity between "historical" symbols and "natural" symbols. In the sense in which I use these terms here, "historical" symbols are those which derive from Christian stories, e.g., a cross (the story of Christ's crucifixion), gathering on Sundays (the stories of the resurrection appearances of Christ), the celebration of Easter as Passover (the First Testament Passover stories), the celebration of Eucharist (the last supper accounts), baptism (stories of the baptism of Christ and Matthew's "great commission" to baptize all nations). "Natural" symbols on the other hand are those which derive from our natural environment (the non-human elements of nature), e.g., the changes of the seasons of the year, flowers, night and day, sun, water. Note that "natural" here does not mean "normal."

A great number of other symbols may be regarded as "cultural" in that they derive from culturally normal human behavior, for example, ways of greeting and departing, postures of being-with, of facing, and of ignoring, actions of love or contempt, movements of respecting or entering into personal space. These "cultural" symbols need to be mentioned but they are not my particular focus of concern just here. The central issue on which I want to focus here concerns rather the relationship between "historical" and "natural" symbols.

There has been a practice in the past of simply transferring without alteration the liturgical calendar as it has developed in the north temperate zone of the Earth to other areas of the planet. This transference becomes an issue once we recognize that the historical symbols of the Christian church have become intertwined with natural symbols of the north temperate zone but that they clash with the natural symbols of other Earth zones.

There are a number of reasons, I think, why this has become an issue at this particular time:

(1) It is no longer assumed that northern, and especially Mediterranean-European, forms of Christianity are definitive, nor that they may be transferred elsewhere without

alteration. The change in this general presupposition about the interactions of gospel and culture affects also the particular case of the liturgical calendar.

(2) In a more ecumenical and culturally sensitive atmosphere, the "Bible only" stance of the European Reformation churches can now be modified with the recognition that Christian gatherings today cannot simply imitate biblical gatherings any more than they can imitate medieval European gatherings. Some inculturation of how, when, and by what symbols Christians gather is necessary and inevitable.

(3) An increased concern with our natural environment calls attention to the part we play in the life of the planet Earth as a whole together with our part in respecting or destroying the integrity of more localized ecosystems. Liturgy in general, and Eucharist in particular, are among the important places where an integration of historical Christianity with endangered natural environments can appropriately take place.

An issue then for Christians outside of the north temperate zone where the traditional liturgical calendar was developed concerns our liturgical use of a calendar which is often at odds with our natural cycles and seasons. There are several different cycles which contribute to the makeup of the liturgical calendar. The issue may be pinpointed more sharply by focusing on two major constituent cycles of the liturgical calendar as it has developed in its northern use: (1) the christological cycle, with, first, Easter and, second, Christmas as its pivotal points; (2) the sanctoral cycle which dots the year with remembrances of saints.

(1) The *christological cycle* has its pivotal points firstly at Easter (with its date calculated according to a combination of cycles relative to both sun and moon—the Sunday after the first full moon following the spring equinox of the northern hemisphere) and secondly at Christmas (with its date calculated according to the cycle of the Earth around the sun—25th December). These pivotal feasts are prepared for by the liturgical seasons of Lent

and Advent respectively, and are maintained over several weeks by the Easter and Christmas liturgical seasons which follow the actual feastdays themselves. The way the occurrences of the Christian Easter and Christmas are calculated need not concern us except to note that in the north temperate zone Easter occurs in spring and Christmas in winter.

Both Easter and Christmas are first and foremost *historical* feasts. Easter remembers the death-resurrection of Christ, and this event is itself dependent for its timing and interpretation upon the historical Jewish feast of Passover. But the Jewish Passover is itself related to earlier *seasonal* rather than historical festivals of spring. Christmas remembers the historical event of the birth of Christ, though its timing in December may possibly, but by no means certainly, be related to mid-winter, i.e., seasonal, festivals. Even though these feasts themselves are primarily historical, a good deal of the symbolism through which they are celebrated derives from the natural seasons, spring and winter, respectively, in which they occur. The spring associations of Easter in the northern temperate zone—unleavened bread, lambs, new life, new light, new growth—are not transferable to tropical zones where spring does not occur nor to the south temperate zone where Easter occurs in autumn. Similarly, many of the midwinter associations of Christmas in the northern temperate zones—snow, cold weather feasting, the shortest days about to lengthen, warmth in the family home—again do not occur in tropical zones and make no sense at all in the south temperate summer. Similarly, the period of Lent as a time of preparation or penitence leading into the spring of new growth and new life, and the period of Advent wreaths surviving in the increasing darkness and cold waiting for their midwinter reversal like humanity waiting for the birth of the Son of God, do not make much sense outside of the north temperate zone.

(2) In the case of the *sanctoral cycle* the issue is not that of the variety of climatic zones of the Earth, but it is at least in one way fundamentally similar to that of the *christological* cycle. Those of us who live outside of the places of historical Christianity find

that for the sanctoral cycle as well as for the christological cycle our historical memory is out of key with our senses. We know the histories of at least some of these saints, but the evidential traces of their lives are somewhere else. We have *stories* about these people, but for the most part we have no *places* where they lived or prayed or died. We can hear about them, but we cannot point to where they were, what they did, what they touched, what they made. The stories about these people thus perform a different function when they lack any concrete earthly embodiment. They are not so much testimonies of the lives of real people, but function rather as moral stories or legends of human-like people not really human like us. A few of these stories have particular impact on our lives because of the particular relevance to us of what they did or what they stood for. But for the most part the celebration of feastdays of unknown people who lived in unknown places makes most of the sanctoral calendar difficult to relate to and overly foreign.

A Way Forward

A way forward in dealing with the issue of the sanctoral cycle is more obvious and more easily proposed than that concerning the christological cycle. I propose then to deal with the *sanctoral* cycle first. The sanctoral cycle is an intertwining of regular patterns of prayer with testimonies of authentically Christian lives. On the one hand a relatively new local church requires testimonies from older churches before it develops its own. And no local church whether new or old can afford to be so self-preoccupied as to ignore the Christian testimonies of other churches. On the other hand, a total overlay of foreign testimonies can maintain a new local church in a state of religious subservience to that foreign locality from which most of its examples of authentic Christian living have been derived.

The way forward by which a new local church could deal with this subservience would involve four tasks:

(1) A pruning of European-generated sanctoral cycles to remove the impression that you have to be foreign to be a saint. A good deal of this happens anyway as many local communities simply ignore most of the saints in current sanctoral cycles.

(2) A change in the process for including a religious ancestor in the sanctoral cycle. Current notions of "sainthood" imply that a saint is a person who has passed God's tests of perfection. We may need to remove the impression that you have to be perfect before you can be liturgically remembered. We are not looking for perfection here but merely for those people whose lives serve in some major ways as Christian testimonies for us.

(3) Being prepared to commemorate and celebrate liturgically those people whose lives do provide such testimony.

(4) As well as persons, looking also for particular *events* that are appropriate for liturgical celebration. This is not quite the same as a strictly "sanctoral" cycle, but it is similar in that liturgical commemorations of some significant events in our local history, like the commemorations of significant people, are particular points of memory and celebration dotted through the annual cycle.

The *christological* cycle needs more extended consideration. It is here in particular that the historical and natural dimensions of our eucharistic symbolism need reexamination. What, if anything, should be done about the clash between the historical and natural symbols of the annual calendar? I shall propose here a response for the south temperate zone only. A liturgical response can be generated only from *within* a climatic zone. Since I live within the south temperate zone, it is from here that I make my liturgical response to this issue. The fact of attempting a response at all however is suggestive that those in the tropical and arctic zones should undertake their own responses in, I would suggest, a similar way but expecting different results. There are currently two fairly clearcut responses to this issue.

One response maintains that in the south temperate zone we should change the liturgical calendar to correspond with the natural annual cycle. Thus Easter should be celebrated in the southern spring (September-October), Christmas should take place at or about the southern winter solstice (21-22 June). Other important feasts and seasons would fall into place relative to these two pivotal feastdays. Basically, this position advocates the correspondence of the liturgical and the natural annual cycles so that Christian feasts supplant or "baptize" earlier non-Christian celebrations of those natural seasons. Or, if we are not happy with the idea of a Christian takeover of pre-Christian festivals, this position does at least promote the correspondence of Easter with spring and Christmas with midwinter. Thus the rich symbolism of the northern annual cycle with its integration of historical symbols (the major events of the life of Christ) and natural symbols (the seasons of the solar year) is maintained. For the south, it is only the timing that is changed—the whole cycle is shifted forward (or backward) six months, and the clash of historical and natural symbols is eliminated.

A second response regards the liturgical calendar as primarily historical. This response questions the currently popular understanding that the Christian liturgical calendar developed around earlier natural or "pagan" seasonal celebrations. The Christian feast of Easter is essentially the celebration of an historical event, even though it may be linked back through the Jewish Passover to a particular connection of the solar and lunar calendars. The *date* of Easter is determined by a natural event. But the *meaning* of the Christian Easter is historical, namely the death and resurrection of Christ, itself rooted in another historical event, namely the Jewish Passover. In this view, the seasons of the year and their natural symbols are peripheral and in the main irrelevant to the Christian liturgical year. They may be ignored in both the northern and southern hemispheres. In that case, a south temperate liturgical calendar would do best simply to ignore natural accretions to the northern liturgical calendar and treat the Christian feasts simply as anniversaries. Like many anniversaries, when the precise dates of the original event were not known, fictitious dates have been arrived at for reasons (practical, seasonal, political, or theological) which seemed appropriate. It is the regular commemoration of these major events of the life of Christ that is important, not the natural seasons in which they occur. These important commemorations provide an appropriate occasion for other contemporary celebrations such as the initiation of new Christians at Easter or family life at Christmas. All these remain the same no matter in which climatic zone of the Earth they are celebrated.

There is a third response which I would here endorse which takes something from each of the above responses.

The difficulty with the first response above is that its most probable result is liturgical chaos. It could perhaps have worked several centuries ago when communications around the Earth were slow. With the modern speed of communication and the growth of mass communications media, several different timings for Easter and Christmas around the world could be chaotic. Moreover there are no clearcut lines which distinguish one climatic zone from another. The north temperate and south temperate zones are clearly distinct one from the other. But it could well become a matter of dispute where either of these merge into the tropical zones or into the arctic and antarctic zones. If we are to learn from past experience in the history of Christianity, church and cultural identities might well collect around disputes on the timing of Easter or Christmas, so that these feasts become an occasion or source of division within Christianity. Even more basically perhaps, it is difficult to see that people in general would now accept such an abrupt change in so established a custom as the timing of Easter and Christmas. All in all, this is too chaotic a solution, and while it solves some problems for local churches which are clearly within the south temperate zone, it is no solution for many other places. Moreover, there still seems to be advantage in having Christians throughout the world celebrating these major feasts at the same time. All in all this solution has too little gain for too much cost.

The second response above also has its problems. The main problem is that it is too much a north temperate response which is happy to regard the liturgical calendar as historical because it does not itself have to suffer the kind of clashing of symbols which occurs in the south temperate and other zones when these feasts are divorced from their natural counterparts in the north. The two kinds of symbolism are not so simply separated. They are not neutral one to the other, and they tend either to cohere or to clash. It is perhaps more obvious in the south that when our historical symbols are divorced from our natural symbols in liturgy, we are pushed toward a view of humanity divorced from its environment and a Christ divorced from creation. Much of the force of this historical argument seems to come from a desire to counter the position that Christian festivals derive from pre-Christian "pagan" festivals at least as to their timing and to some of their symbolism. But the force of such argument is greatly diminished in cultures where such contests did not occur at all, or did not occur in that way, or whose timing was different.

A third solution, then, is to treat the Christian feasts as *primarily but not only historical*. In this case, the key Christian feast of Easter is treated as the anniversary of the death and resurrection of Christ regardless of the season or the point in the natural cycle when it originally occurred. Since we do not know the actual date of the birth of Christ, a traditional fictitious date for Christmas is quite acceptable regardless of the original reasons for settling on that date. It is an entirely different thing however to claim, then, that our liturgy ought to operate quite independently of the natural symbols, our environment, through which we understand God, our world, and ourselves.

The northern liturgical calendar has developed a coherence between the historical Christian symbols and those of their natural environment with its annual seasons. The south needs to do the same. But the natural symbols will not be the same for the southern as they are for the northern hemisphere. The rewards for developing such a new and different coherence are likely to be new light on the traditional Christian feasts and their seasons, and the possibility of new kinds of relationship to God. According to the natural seasons on which we celebrate these anniversaries we will begin to notice a coherence between these feasts and our natural world which will serve to illustrate, to reverse, to unveil our understanding of God. The process is similar to that already undertaken in the north, but its results will be different.

What Are the Theological Principles at Issue Here?

(1) Local and universal church.

The sanctoral and christological liturgical cycles each confront us, though in somewhat different ways, with a basic theological decision. Let us look first here at the *sanctoral* cycle. The theological decision confronting us in the sanctoral cycle is one we encountered in previous chapters. It concerns the local and universal dimensions of the Christian community. These two dimensions are not in contradiction. We would expect a Christian community to be *both* local *and* universal. The difficulty is to establish just where the balance between these two dimensions lies. And in practice if not in principle, our decisions about this do often leave us with an imbalance and even conflict. We have already been alerted to this in the cases of liturgical leadership, inclusive language and language relevance. The sanctoral cycle faces us with a similar self-examination and a similar theological decision.

Testimonies to Christian living from our past seem such innocent, unquestionably good affairs surely not requiring searching discernment. Yet the lives of those we regard as martyrs and saints function as powerful commentaries on the gospel. They are among the most appealing and memorable ways of translating the impact of the life of Christ across ages and across cultures. They are also among the most appealing and memorable ways of grossly distorting and misinterpreting the life of Christ. They provide us with models of behavior which ethical explanation and spiritual exhortation cannot match for vividness and immediacy. An intransigent colonial Christianity will find the vivid presentation of its own saints, and the expectation that its new converts will imitate them, as among the most effective knots in its apron-strings. The most myopically self-centered local church will find effective self-reinforcement in the constant meditation on its own local saints and heroes to the exclusion of any examples of holiness, charity and courage from anywhere else.

Moreover, every local Christian community, even a relatively new one, needs to deal with its own history either in convenient forgetting or in careful discernment of fidelity and tragedy. If its only attitude toward its own past is forgetfulness, then its identity is open for takeover by whatever interest groups see advantage in doing so. Alternatively, it can seek to discern in its own history who were the goodies, who were the baddies, and who belonged to the various grades in between. It can seek to discern which events in its history are worth celebrating, which are worth lamenting, and which may simply be forgotten. Contentment with a sanctoral cycle which contains no local saints nor local events means that we have left these decisions to be made elsewhere. We have no common reflection upon nor common discernment about our past, and probably no capacity to evaluate our present. The development of a local sanctoral cycle thus rests upon a theological decision to take responsibility for our own local history while at the same time learning from the testimonies of other churches, especially from the older, more traditional Christian communities throughout the world.

(2) Our coherence within God's creation.

A second theological decision, and one that we have not so far encountered in this examination of issues in eucharistic symbolism, confronts us more particularly in the *christological* cycle of the liturgical calendar. The current practice maintains throughout the world the calendar developed in the north. This practice subjects the Earth's variety of seasons, ecosystems, and climates to a fictitious uniformity. Advocated solutions propose either altering the timing of Easter and Christmas in other Earth zones to fit in with the Earth's seasons, or ignoring the Earth's seasons altogether and following a purely historical interpretation of the liturgical calendar. The approach which I have advocated above maintains the current timing of the christological cycle but seeks also to develop a southern calendar in tune with the natural southern seasons. This approach is initially historical but wants also to integrate the christological cycle into the complex relationships between human beings and their natural environment. This approach goes further than merely making a case for a *local* Christianity in distinction from trans-cultural versions of Christianity. What is specific about the argument for a local version of a *christological* liturgical cycle, over and above the argument for a local version of a *sanctoral* cycle, is that it is not concerned just with the relationships between one local church and another, but is concerned specifically with human relationships to and within the planet Earth.

The point at issue here is perhaps best expressed as a difference between a liturgical practice which seeks God almost entirely in the events of *human* history, and a liturgical practice which seeks God in an *Earth* history. If we opt for the latter, warning lights of "paganism" and "syncretism" begin to flash. Are we here reducing Christianity to a "cosmic" or "nature" religion and betraying the incarnation of God's word as the central belief of Christianity? It is appropriate that some warning lights should flash here because such betrayal has occurred in the past and could occur again for us. But are we then to concentrate our symbolism so exclusively on the human person of Christ that both Christ and ourselves somehow cease to exist within the larger reality of the Earth which is also God's face or God's body? The reality of Christ, the word of God, is not just a human reality but also an Earth reality.

A theology which is concerned only with God's relation to human beings, or is concerned exclusively with human salvation, but ignores the rest of God's creation contributes to an instrumental view of the Earth. It allows the Earth to be exploited for human purposes and treats it without the respect due to its creator. Yet there is a strong liturgical tradition which treats the Earth, its elements and its seasons, with respect as symbols of God's care and God's awesomeness, of God's immanence and God's transcendence, of God's intimacy and God's power.

Here, then, is the theological position which underlies our approach to the christological cycle of the liturgical calendar. The proposal I make here for a south temperate version of the annual christological cycle, rests on a theological position which adopts an Earth-centered rather than a purely human-centered approach to our relationship to God. It sees the whole of creation, and in particular as far as we Earth creatures are concerned, the whole of the planet Earth with its cycles and seasons and ecosystems and variety, as symbols of God's presence. It is prepared to risk the dangers of "paganism" for the rewards of richness and variety in our symbols of God.

We need to notice, though, that if we adopt the position I have advocated above, then we have made a theological choice. For there is an alternative theological position which wants to focus in a much more concentrated way on the human reality of the word of God. The consequence of such a concentrated focus is a liturgy which emphasizes the historical symbols of God's presence and deemphasizes or even rejects the natural symbols of God's presence. It will thus tend either to disregard entirely the annual liturgical cycle or else to treat its annual liturgical festivals as anniversaries of historical events unrelated to the natural environment.

What Are the Practical Liturgical Effects?

A *sanctoral* cycle appropriate for more recently founded local churches will normally require some uncluttering of inherited sanctoral cycles in the sense of removing those saints for whom no clear relevance can be established for the local church. A sanctoral cycle cluttered with unknown and meaningless saints weakens the effect of remembering significant people whose lives give testimony to the Holy Spirit in our history.

More importantly and more positively the development of an appropriate sanctoral cycle requires that we actively seek out those of our religious ancestors whose life-testimonies do indeed provide us with examples of authentic Christian living.

Interwoven with the sanctoral cycle, similar to it in that it is secondary to the major annual celebrations of the life of Christ, but dissimilar in that it focuses on events rather than individual people, is an "event" cycle. These liturgically celebrated events of local significance are important in constituting the identity of the local Christian community and its relationship to the history of the society. The liturgical celebration of events, unlike the liturgical celebration of saints, does not require any decision about holiness. Events may be lamented as well as glorified, they may call for repentance as much as for thanksgiving. Many communities will find it more congenial to remember liturgically their significant events rather than to have to decide upon the sainthood of particular individuals in all the ambiguity of an individual's life. Whether in the case of past events or of deceased people, the decision for inclusion in a liturgical calendar does require a process of discernment with a sharp sensitivity to the various personal, familial, tribal, and political interests which may want their own people or events glorified or praised.[1]

The sanctoral cycle operates in the main on weekdays rather than Sundays. Let us turn now to the *christological* cycle which operates in the main at the Sunday Eucharist.

I have proposed above that among the options for an appropriate south temperate liturgical cycle is that of retaining the current timing of the pivotal feasts and liturgical seasons but reinterpreting them in terms of the natural seasons in which they occur. This has several effects:

---

[1] In Aotearoa New Zealand, the Anglican *A New Zealand Prayer Book: He Karakia Mihinare o Aotearoa* (Auckland: William Collins, 1989, pp. 10–13) includes a substantial contribution to the development of a local calendar. It includes some events of national significance as well as commemorations of "people who have provided inspiration and an example of Christian living in the history of this country, or who have contributed to the development of Christianity in this country."

(1) It maintains a symbolic expression of the universality of Christianity in its common timing of its major feasts.

(2) It puts us liturgically in contact with the larger sphere of God's creation rather than merely the particular flow of human history.

(3) It forces us to rethink the major events of the life of Christ and our current living in Christ's Spirit in ways which highlight new aspects and greater richness in our glimpses of the mystery of God. Thus:

(a) Christmas: Festival of life (December 25th: Summer solstice).

The feast of the birth of Christ takes place at a time of full daylight and strong benevolent sun. This is a temperate sun. Not a distant sun struggling to shine through cloud and snow! Not a desert-making sun which withers and burns! This is a sun which wraps all living things in warmth and light. A sun at the peak of spring growth but not yet at the dryness of late summer. The plants and newborn animals are full of energy, of extravagant unmeasured strength. The shades of green are strong and varied. Colors are everywhere. People spend more time outside in the fresh early mornings, the warm days, and the long cool evenings. The birth of a child comes like a bright human flowering to crown a long preparation and growth in the biosphere. God's power and beauty, the sap of the living Earth, has broken forth in many ways in days past, and now bursts through again in a Godlike child. This is a time of gratitude for life in all its variety, for newness and innocence and children, and especially for God's own child, the promise of what is yet to be.

Yet now in our times, this thanksgiving and hope in the energy of the sun is touched with fear. In our times the sun is not so benevolent as it used to be. Human excess has thinned the ozone layer and the ultraviolet rays can be deadly. The death-dealing ways of human disrespect have tainted with death the benevolence of the temperate sun, source of energy and life, just as the human child of God was born under the fear of the dealers in death who had no room for such a child.

(b) Advent: Season of hope and promise.

Advent is the four-week preparation for Christmas. It is not a season of increasing winter. It is a season of the exuberant growth of spring. The scripture readings in Advent are about expectation, an ambiguous and multilayered expectation. They are a memory of looking forward, and a looking forward in memory. They remember how the people of Israel looked forward to a Messiah and especially John the Baptist's preparation for that Messiah. They also look forward to a future fulfilment for us based on the memory of Jesus of Nazareth's own beginning of a reign of God on Earth, an eternal life lived in flesh and in resurrection.

In a spring Advent the manifestation of this eternal life, this regenerative life-giving power of God is all around us and through us. God does not need here to "intervene" in the affairs of Earth and its people to reverse the increasing power of darkness. This regenerative life is already here. We have only to be faithful to it, to be immersed within it, and wait for it to become a human yet still Godlike extravagance. Advent is a chrysalis time, a time of pregnancy. It produces what is expected and hoped for; yet what it produces is beyond expectation and too much to hope for, so that at the end we will be left mainly with wonder.

(c) Easter: Festival of darkness and meantime (April: After the autumn equinox).

Easter is a festival of death. It is a time of increasing darkness, darkness of spirit and darkness over the Earth. Good Friday dominates Holy Week. It is a memory of inhumanity, a memory of tragedy, lightened a little by the pale presence of the full moon. There is a threat about autumn. The Easter candle shines in the darkness. But it is such a little light, and it does not dispel the darkness. The celebration of the resurrection of Christ is not the fulfillment of God's reign on Earth. It is only the beginning of the meantime. It is time for growth in darkness. Many things happen in darkness. Seeds are nurtured within the soil. Roots grow beneath the earth. It is not a time for sight. For us now, in the south it is not a time for visions and appearances. It is a time for Earth's creatures less dependent on the sense of sight. It is a time for listening and hearing, for groping and touching. It is a time for faith's commitments rather than for clearly sighted landmarks. It is a meantime of resurrection. This resurrection is an immersion into our Earth origin, a disappearance beyond vision. Resurrection is not a fantasy, it is a meantime. Here Christ's resurrection is not the first-fruit, it is a seed planted, a seed in a tomb. Everything still looks the same, but this is not a time for seeing, and in the meantime everything is changing. In the meantime we wait, we listen, we grope, and we sense in faith's darkness.

(d) Lent: Season of many deaths.

Lent is preparation for Easter. The reds and golds of autumn give conflicting hints of blood and fire and splendor. Yet it is a time of increasing coldness and lessening light. Leaves fall, little things dying. Lent is a time of catechumenate, a time for a change of heart, when little by little we shed the idols and the selfishness that we have accumulated over the years. It is a time, too, for a return to earlier, clearer, and purer commitments. It is a time for letting things die that need to die. It is a letting go of accumulated baggage however useful or attractive. It is preparation for the festival of death, the time of trial when in the face of crucifixion only one commitment finally counts.

Not all things die nor need to die, however. Along with autumn's little deaths, life still flowers and ripens after the heat of midsummer. Autumn is not yet winter, but it is colder now and we need to give attention to conserving our resources, to check and prune extravagance. No need now for flowers in church, for bright colors in clothing or banners or cloths. Let the mood of autumn filter into our liturgies. It is not a mood for extravagance but a mood for enough, for taking stock.

(e) The ordinary Sundays of the year.

The pivotal feasts and seasons centered around Christmas and Easter are only part of the liturgical year. We need not, and

probably should not, interpret the whole of the gospel through
the lenses of the natural cycle of the Earth. The "ordinary"
Sundays of the year provide the majority of Sundays in which
our liturgy of the word focuses, for the most part, on the theology
of one of the gospels. Here it is not the natural season that first
attracts our attention, but the gradual unravelling of a gospel's
perspective on God's revelation in Jesus of Nazareth. This does
not mean that we ignore the rest of God's creation and revelation
by focusing on one human person. The humanity of Christ is a
humanity within the Earth not apart from nor in spite of it. The
scriptures constantly call our attention to God's creation, greater
than and more encompassing than human beings. Sunday after
Sunday through the ordinary part of the liturgical year we are
required to proclaim a good news about God and the whole of
God's creation, not merely a human-centered gospel.

The pivotal feasts of Christmas and Easter have traditionally
called Christian attention to the natural seasons within which
they occur. In Earth zones outside the one in which the interconnections between Christian history and the natural seasons
were developed, these interconnections have to be broken and
rewoven. Christmas and Easter and their associated liturgical
seasons are the major times when this reweaving can take place.
This does not mean we abandon the ordinary Sundays of the
year to merely human historical interpretation. It means that
having had our attention reworked and widened at Christmas
and Easter we can now understand and ritualize and live out the
gospel messages of each Sunday's Eucharist in a creation-cen-
tered and not merely human-centered understanding of God.

Beyond Liturgy

The effect of working toward a local sanctoral and event cycle
in the liturgical calendar contributes to a local church taking
responsibility for its own history not isolated from, but in combination with, the larger history of the universal church.

The practice of a regular Eucharist which integrates historical and natural symbols acts as a point of integration of historical Christianity and contemporary ecological concerns. It contributes to an ethically responsible view of the human role within God's Earth.

Chapter 5

With Whom and How Often to Celebrate Eucharist

The Issue

The question *with whom* to celebrate Eucharist, and the question *how often* to celebrate Eucharist, are distinct questions but quite closely interrelated. Let us begin with the question of "with whom."

It may seem strange to ask this question at all. Shouldn't we be prepared to celebrate Eucharist with anyone? Are we to pick and choose between people and exclude some while including others? Is it narrow-minded and exclusivist even to ask such a question?

Yet most of us make choices all the time about those with whom we celebrate Eucharist. I do not refer here to the occasional foray into something different or a tourist-like interest in liturgies that are exotic and mind-broadening. I refer here to our regular normal participation in Eucharist where we know some or most of the people there and we have fairly well-established expectations of what will occur there. Most of us commonly have a choice of several Eucharists in which we could participate as well as the choice of not taking part at all. In fact we choose one rather than others or decide against all of them. This does not mean we are particularly prejudiced or narrow-minded. It usually means much simpler things, such as that one Eucharist is closer than others, or that one Eucharist is in our own language, or that one Eucharist more than others is in a style in which we find it easier to participate, or that one Eucharist more than others takes our particular age group into account, or that one rather than others caters for young families. Or sometimes the reasons behind our choice may be a little more complex and a little more intense. There may be things occurring in a particular Eucharist with which we disagree. Sexist language, irrelevant language, domination of the Eucharist by one person, contradictions between what people profess at Eucharist and their behavior outside of Eucharist are things that might lead us to avoid, or take part in, one Eucharist rather than another.

In all these cases we are making choices about *with whom* we celebrate Eucharist. Symbols do not occur on their own. They occur as communicative acts among people. If gender-inclusive language occurs in Eucharist, it does so because people have decided to be gender-inclusive. If we choose to be at a Eucharist in which gender-inclusive language is used we make a choice to be with these people rather than with people who do not do so. If we take part in an English-language Eucharist rather than a Tongan-language Eucharist, it is usually because we understand more easily, communicate more easily, pray more easily in English than in Tongan. Because of our language limitations we communicate more easily with English-speakers than with Tongan-speakers. Sometimes we may, of course, take part in a Tongan-speaking Eucharist just to broaden our own understanding or because we have friends there. But in any case we are constantly choosing those *with whom* we celebrate Eucharist for a whole variety of reasons mostly to do with communication and belief but sometimes exposing prejudice and discrimination.

We should note, too, that the issue of *with whom* to celebrate Eucharist is not just a modern question. It is also a traditional one. Eucharist is a sign of unity among Christians. This is a readily acknowledged understanding of the meaning of Eucharist. We do not, however, give quite so much acknowledgement to its converse. Eucharist *also* operates as a sign of *schism*. Or perhaps we can express this in a more nuanced way by saying that Eucharist expresses not only the unity of Christians, but also legitimate pluralism among Christians, as well as unreconciled differences among Christians. Unity implies the actual or possible celebration of Eucharist together. Legitimate pluralism implies that Eucharist is actually celebrated separately but that it is possible to celebrate it together at any time. Unreconciled difference implies that Eucharist is actually celebrated separately and that celebration together is not regarded as possible. The healing of a schism implies the celebration of Eucharist again together.

In this light, the contemporary issue of with whom to celebrate Eucharist may be divided into three aspects:

(1) *Ecumenism.* The term "ecumenism" as it is normally used theologically and liturgically is concerned with reconciling past separations among Christians. This is a reconciling between Christian denominations. It proceeds according to (a) the willingness to reorder priorities among *beliefs* and sometimes to change beliefs, (b) the willingness to heal or forget *memories* of historical injustices of one church toward another; (c) the development of a common *symbolism* so that people from various denominations can feel at home at, can belong to, can identify with, can fully participate in common worship.

(2) *Liturgical communication.* The contemporary issue of *with whom* to celebrate Eucharist is not solely to do with relationships between Christian denominations. It is also to do with the possibilities of communication across sociocultural barriers. Three factors in particular are important in enabling or hindering liturgical communication: (a) *Language*, in the specific sense of English, Spanish, Maori, Vietnamese, etc. (b) *Ritual style*, in the sense that different cultures use their bodies in different ways in ritual, e.g. an emphasis on actions in unison on the one hand or on idiosyncratic freedom on the other, an emphasis on controlled body language or on enthusiastic exuberance, an emphasis on singing or on silence. (c) *Life-style* outside of liturgy but carried into liturgy in the many signals of socioeconomic and cultural identity such as dress, means of travel, hairstyle, color, accent.

(3) *Discrimination.* The above two factors imply a certain pluralism, an acceptance of differences in belief and liturgical communication. The live-and-let-live philosophy of pluralism tends,
however, to conceal injustice. Some liturgical symbolism may be
not merely a matter of legitimate pluralism signalling differing
historical or cultural styles, but indeed a matter of right and
wrong. In a liturgical context, this is not merely a matter of
something being wrong in an abstract sense, but of *wrong done to*
one or other sector of the community. The issues discussed in
the previous chapters of this book, namely, leadership, language
and natural symbols, have all been matters of this sort. When
differences in liturgical symbolism are regarded not as matters
of legitimate pluralism but as matters of justice, this signals that
the issue is not merely a matter of agreement to be different but
is rather a matter of perceived discrimination. In this case it has
raised for at least one of the parties the question of *with whom*
Eucharist should be celebrated.

At this point I propose to focus the issue more clearly by
adopting one particular aspect of Eucharist as a kind of standard. It then becomes possible to examine alternatives and differences in terms of this standard. Such a standard is like setting
a center line so that we can then describe various positions as a
certain distance to the left of, or to the right of, or right on top of,
that center line. As in driving a car on the road, the center line is
not necessarily the best place to be. It does serve, though, to set
out the options relative to one another.

Such standards are to some degree arbitrary. But there is a standard which is sanctioned by tradition. This standard is the traditional ideal of the *local* Eucharist. The ideal of the local Eucharist
is that all Christians within a geographical area take part in the
same Sunday Eucharist. This ideal can seldom be achieved in
practice unless the Christians of a geographical area have a lot of
things in common in addition to their being Christian (no language differences, no socioeconomic differences, no ethnic differences, no migrants, complete accord on age and gender, status
and roles, etc.). Nevertheless, the ideal of the local Sunday

Eucharist serves as a standard in reference to which we can attend to the major kinds of variety affecting the Eucharist of a local Christian community. In attending to these major kinds of variety we attend also to the principal points at which the issues of identity (of *with whom* to celebrate Eucharist) arise.

Any local church will have its own major kinds of variety. In the church with which I am most familiar, the following factors produce major variances from the standard of the *local* community Eucharist.:

(1) *Church denomination:* Over time, whatever their origins, church denominations have developed their own styles of organization and liturgy. These differences are ones that most of us have grown up with and with which we are familiar. Among the variances discussed here, these denominational ones are probably the most consciously recognized and discussed. The beliefs and social practices which originated these differences have largely disappeared into history. People are becoming more familiar with, and therefore more at home in, the liturgies of other Christian denominations. Nevertheless, loyalty to a particular church denomination remains an important element in Christian identity. For most people, "local" church is still more likely to mean the local church of *my denomination* than a strictly local church encompassing all Christians within that locality.

(2) *Culture:* The three dimensions of liturgical communication that I have listed above, namely, language, ritual style, and the indicators of life-style, may vary considerably from one culture to another. Where people from different cultures live in the same local Christian community, the different kinds of liturgical communication are rarely simply pluralist. Issues of liturgical pluralism move quite quickly into issues of justice as one culture becomes liturgically dominant over the others.

(3) *Gender:* Whether within the same culture or across cultures, most Christian communities carry a liturgical history in which the liturgical symbols signal that women are peripheral

or subordinate within the liturgical action. As a result of this history, most contemporary local communities are currently in the throes of dealing with gender inequality within liturgy.

(4) *Age:* As with cultures, so also generations tend to differ in their preferred kind of liturgical communication. It is seldom that a single Eucharist can be said to have communicated satisfactorily among children, the youth, the young adults, the middle aged, and the elderly. Eucharistic symbolism does not often signal age equality. More often one or several of those generations is dealt with as peripheral to the liturgical action.

(5) *Internal elitism:* The most common form of elitism internal to the church itself is that which we usually call "clericalism." The mere fact of having liturgical leaders, and even full-time leaders, does not in itself constitute elitism. Elitism occurs when some liturgical leaders control the liturgical communication in such a way that both communal participation and other ministries are disabled. Rather than empowerment, leadership in this case becomes disablement for other participants.

(6) *Golden-age loyalties:* These are a attachments to a "golden age" of liturgy in the sense that a perception of how Eucharist was celebrated during one era in the past is considered to be ideal. In comparison to the liturgical style of this golden age, all other styles of liturgical communication are considered inferior.

It is not the mere fact of variety itself that is the issue here. The variations from the "local church" standard occur because of the difficulty in achieving equality or due proportion among the different sectors of the local community within the symbolism of the local Eucharist. In many cases the actual symbolism of the local Eucharist is unable to cope with this variety. What often results is not due liturgical recognition of variety within the local community, but the establishment of relationships of centrality-peripherality, or more seriously, relationships of domination-subordination between the various sectors of that local community. Such relationships distort the symbolism of Eucharist. It is the attempt to escape from or to correct such distorted symbolism that causes the most acute difficulties about *with whom* one can satisfactorily and honestly celebrate Eucharist.

In summary, then, the issue of with whom to celebrate Eucharist focuses most acutely on the point where differences in liturgical communication become matters of discrimination. These precise points may vary from one part of the world to another. In my reading of the local church most familiar to me, these points of focus may be listed as follows:

(1) Where one church tradition does not seek eucharistic communion with another.
(2) Where one culture excludes others from liturgical expression.
(3) Where one gender marginalizes the other in liturgical expression.
(4) Where one age group dominates liturgical expression.
(5) Where an elite leadership disempowers other church members from liturgical expression.
(6) Where preference for one "golden age" of liturgical expression disallows any other forms of liturgy.

So far I have been concerned with the question of with whom to celebrate Eucharist. This has led me to focus on the issue of discrimination in the six forms listed above. Thus far, then, I have considered only the first half of the initial question which makes up the heading of this chapter. Let us turn now to the second half of the initial question, that is, to the issue of *how often* to celebrate Eucharist. There are a number of questions which need to be worked through briefly here before we settle on a central focus. I shall deal with these in a series of points.

(1) *Regularity.* How regularly should we celebrate Eucharist? The question of regularity arises partly for historical reasons because of different practices within the various streams of Christian tradition. In recent history the regularity of Eucharist

has varied between the Catholic and Orthodox practice of daily Eucharist and the Presbyterian practice of quarterly, i.e., four times a year, Eucharist. The practice of "open" communion, the lessening of an over-reverential attitude toward Eucharist, an emphasis on the liturgy of the word within the overall structure of Eucharist, are all recent movements within the churches which contribute to diminishing the rationale for a *less*-than-weekly Eucharist. While there remain questions of practice and tradition for some churches, the rationale for a less-than-weekly Eucharist is less cogent than it used to be. The rationale for a *more*-than-weekly, i.e., daily, Eucharist usually recognizes that Sunday Eucharist and a daily Eucharist each have somewhat different functions in the Christian community. The Sunday Eucharist gathers, or attempts to gather, the whole community. It thus plays a much more important role in the Christian community than does the daily Eucharist. Except in the case of some residential religious communities, weekday Eucharists rarely attempt to gather more than a small fraction of the Sunday assembly.

I shall adopt the position here that our major concern needs to be focused on the *weekly Sunday* Eucharist. This position includes the assumption that Eucharist is the normal form of the Sunday gathering of Christians.

(2) *Occasions.* So far I have been concerned only to clear the way through some of the questions to do with the regularity of Eucharist. I have settled on the regular Sunday (i.e., weekly, rather than daily, or monthly, or quarterly) Eucharist as our focus. In addition to regularity, the other kind of frequency questions concerning Eucharist are to do with occasions. "Occasional" Eucharists are those which occur not simply from within the daily, weekly, or monthly patterns of cyclic time, but because of some particular reason or purpose. Such occasions are of four main kinds:

(a) special times within the christological or sanctoral calendars (e.g., Christmas, Easter, special saints' days);

(b) special events in individual, familial, or civic life (e.g., weddings, funerals, national holidays);
(c) special-purpose gatherings of Christians (e.g., conferences, rallies, meetings, retreats);
(d) non-regular gatherings of Christians where the special purpose is the Eucharist itself.

Such occasions for Eucharist carry their own special questions, the most acute of which are to do with who takes part—what kind of Christian identity is implied in the Christmas and Easter only attender, or whether to have a Eucharist at a wedding when most of the people present are not Christians. In a pluralist society should national festivals be celebrated with Eucharist or some more inclusive ceremonial or both? etc. These questions, therefore, lead us back into the "with whom" style of questions. As far as "how often" questions are concerned, *occasional* Eucharists may be said to constitute the lowest common denominator in the sense that Eucharist on special occasions only is just one step up from no Eucharist at all. The issues about how often arise only once we seek something more than the minimal position of Eucharist for special occasions.

(3) *Church attendance.* Sometimes discussions to do with the frequency of Eucharist turn into discussions about how to get more people to attend more often or more regularly. Although this is a matter of concern in many communities it is not the point at issue here. The issue on which we focus here is strictly to do with the eucharistic symbolism itself, i.e., the communicative acts which occur within the Eucharist liturgy, not with a campaign to get more people there. It may very well be, and probably is the case, that if we can get the symbolism right it will be less exclusive of those who should genuinely be there. On the other hand it may also turn away people who are currently regular participants because the new symbols carry messages which they are not used to or which they do not like. Thus getting the symbolism right does not predict that there will be an increase in the number of participants. Symbolism is not just

about being there, it is about what happens, and what happens *to* you, when you're there.

(4) *Leaders and participants.* Finally, in this initial exercise of sorting out what we have to deal with and where we need to focus, we need to take into account a distinction between (a) the responsibility of church leaders to *ensure the occurrence of* Eucharist, and (b) the responsibility of Christians to *participate in* Eucharist. We might maintain, for example, that Christians need to participate in Sunday Eucharists only occasionally but at the same time maintain that church leaders have a responsibility to provide for Eucharist to occur every Sunday. Or again, we might maintain that there is a Christian responsibility to participate in Eucharist regularly on Sundays, but that in some places church leaders may be unable or unwilling to provide competent personnel. I use the term "church leaders" here in a quite broad sense to refer to all those who have responsibility for the liturgical life of the community. Some of these may be ordained ministers and others may not be. Some will be members of the local community and some will have wider responsibility at the national or international level for liturgical texts, rubrics, and organization.

There are two issues in particular that we need to give brief attention to here concerning the responsibility of church leaders to ensure the occurrence of Eucharist. One of these issues occurs because of an *overly strong* sense of responsibility on the part of church leaders. In its extreme form this responsibility appears as a desire to ensure simply *that Eucharist occurs at all*—however badly. This entails making sure that an ordained minister, however competent or incompetent, is at the right place and time to accomplish the words and actions of Eucharist, but apart from this no further issues of symbolism need be considered. The responsibility that is accepted in this case is a responsibility for the occurrence of Eucharist rather than a responsibility toward the Christian community itself. It is a responsibility toward the eucharistic action rather than toward the eucharistic assembly. The second issue to which we need to give brief attention here is in some ways the opposite of the first. It is the issue of an *overly weak* sense of responsibility on the part of church leaders. In its extreme form this lack of responsibility allows communities to go without Eucharist because of a lack of ordained ministers. Since wherever there is a Christian community there are always candidates for ordained ministry, the lack of ordained ministers is a result of criteria for ordination which no member of that community can meet. The responsibility that is accepted by church leaders in this case is a responsibility toward the quality of ordained ministers, rather than a responsibility to ensure the occurrence of Eucharist within the community.

Both aspects of this issue of responsibility in church leadership are important. They need to be dealt with in their own place, but they do not fall within the central focus on issues in *symbolism*. Both of these aspects of responsibility, one due to over-enthusiasm and the other due to under-enthusiasm for the occurrence of Eucharist, are a result of insufficient attention to the symbolism itself of Eucharist. They pay attention primarily in the one case to the *sheer presence* of the ordained minister and in the other to the *desirable qualities* of an ordained minister, but they avoid giving attention to the whole complex of symbols which constitute a Eucharist.

I proposed above a distinction between the responsibility of church leaders to ensure the occurrence of Eucharist and the responsibility of Christians to participate in Eucharist. I have tried to clear away some of the questions concerning the responsibility of church leaders. But it is the second part of this distinction, i.e., *the responsibility of Christians to participate in* Eucharist, that needs to occupy our central focus. We can already give a preliminary answer to the question, "how often," by saying, *"normally every Sunday."* This is a standard, conventional and wholly expected response. I do not consider this to be problematic as a general norm. That is to say, the central issue becomes obvious once we have accepted this general norm.

This central issue may then be formulated as follows: What is to be said of Sunday Eucharists in which the symbolism is so distorted, that is, it contains so much discrimination in the form of exclusion and irrelevance, that it might be better not to participate than to participate? It is here in particular that "how often" intersects with "with whom" because failure to solve the issues of discrimination in eucharistic symbolism render all questions of frequency indefinitely problematic.

A Way Forward

Let us begin by looking at four commonly proposed, but in my opinion mistaken, ways forward. I shall then propose a fifth way which I consider to be the most satisfactory one.

(1) *The way of exhortation.*

Exhortation to tolerance, pluralism, and mutual respect is a common way of dealing with the proposal that current eucharistic symbolism is discriminatory. This is the use of persuasive discourse in an appeal for peace and harmony within the community. It is a method commonly resorted to by church leaders who see their responsibility as primarily toward unity within the community. In its use of persuasive discourse, however, this method ignores the variety of liturgical symbolism itself and the power of that very symbolism to influence people's lives. The symbolism of Eucharist, apart from the exhortation itself, is here treated as if it were value free. The great variety of symbols which occur during a Eucharist are treated as if they were ineffective—an odd position for liturgical planners and performers to adopt. Exhortation on its own is an attempt to persuade people to accept the current eucharistic symbolism regardless of its defects on the basis that this symbolism doesn't really matter anyway. Dissatisfaction with current eucharistic symbols is here treated as something which has gone wrong in people's heads or emotions and it avoids the possibility that there may be something wrong with the eucharistic symbols themselves.

I propose rather that issues in the symbolism of Eucharist have to be treated precisely as issues in symbolism rather than as issues in people's heads or emotions which can be changed by persuasive discourse while leaving unchanged the whole complex of symbols in which those discriminations occur.

(2) The way of personal comfort.

There is a second and again fairly common way of dealing with defects in eucharistic symbolism which is seldom adopted by church leaders but is frequently enough adopted by participants. This method consists simply of participating only or mostly in Eucharists where we feel personally comfortable and avoiding those Eucharists in which we are not comfortable. That is to say, we participate in Eucharists with people who are like us or whom we like. The Eucharist among friends, the Eucharist at a live-in seminar or retreat, and the Eucharist within a homogeneous local community are of this kind.

I would propose, however, that this is too individualistic a solution and that the question "with whom" to celebrate Eucharist has here been answered too simply and too easily. If this is the only kind of Eucharist in which we normally participate, we have become an in-group, a self-centered church or a self-centered person, content with ourselves, unself-critical and with no mission to the rest of the world. This is an over-simple, too self-centered and too comfortable resolution of the issue.

(3) The way of moral purity.

A third strategy for dealing with perceived discrimination or defects in Eucharistic symbolism consists in a resolution not in terms of the most comfortable solution, but in terms of the most *just* solution. The issues of discrimination are here resolved by celebrating Eucharist only with those with whom we agree (or who agree with us) on issues of justice. If, for example, the local community does not accept shared leadership in Eucharist, then I refuse to participate in their Eucharist and will participate only in Eucharists of those communities which do practice shared leadership. Similarly, if a Eucharist includes sexist language I will not take part in it. Or again, I will participate only in those

Eucharists which use my language or which include the symbols of my culture.

It is more difficult to be critical of this strategy than it is of the strategies of exhortation and of personal comfort since in the end moral purity in our symbolism is one of the major goals of liturgical planning and reform. There are, however, two principal dangers which lead us to surround this strategy with cautions. The first is that most of us detect discrimination from where we ourselves are standing. Only sometimes does detection of one form of discrimination sensitize us to other forms of discrimination, and, where it does, the second form is often seen through the lenses of the first. The danger here, then, is that the line demarcating those with whom we do or do not celebrate Eucharist may be determined by a single issue. The second danger is that we develop a liturgical moral elite. The problem, then, is not within liturgy but within our moral responsibility to the majority of people for whom our moral purity is unintelligible or unattainable. In achieving moral purity in liturgical symbolism we have ourselves become defective in our responsibility toward the whole community. In both these cases, we have lost the idea of the *local* church and its responsibility toward the wider society. A way forward needs to maintain the tension between the desire for moral purity and the desire for catholicity, rather than simply to resolve the tension by a total option for moral purity.

(4) The way of loyalty.

A fourth strategy for dealing with discriminatory elements in eucharistic symbolism is that of opting for what we regard as the "essence" of Eucharist and turning a blind eye to defects in its symbolism. This option consists in remaining loyal to the tradition we have inherited or, more specifically, to the church institution which maintains order and continuity. The continuance of Christian belief, the continuance of the Christian church, and the continuing eucharistic presence of God among us have priority, and we are not prepared to jeopardize these even if there are recognizable defects in the symbolism of Eucharist.

A strategy which tries to set its priorities among the inevitably defective liturgies of the church again deserves respect. But this strategy leaves us in the end defenseless against those very defects. If we are not continually sensitive to defects within the church, to the need for continual reform, and especially to the power of defective symbols to conceal God from us, we are eventually left only with loyalty to our defective images of God and perhaps therefore to false gods. Loyalty on its own is insufficient. There is no Eucharist without symbolism, and defective symbolism means distorted beliefs and a discriminatory church. In the end, and if unchecked, this is a church which God abandons.

(5) *The way of negotiation.*

The previously presented ways forward each have their own merit. I have suggested criticisms to each, however, which identify them as mistakes unless radically changed or combined with other strategies. I want to propose now a way forward which seems to me to be the most satisfactory way of proceeding. This way forward may be named the way of "negotiation" from its foundation on the following principles:

(a) *All liturgy contains some distortion.* It is unlikely that we can ever achieve a completely undistorted Eucharist. One of the goals, however, of liturgical action is that of working toward a Eucharist which contains as little distortion as possible. We should attempt to eliminate distortion from our Eucharists as much as possible. This is, nevertheless, an ongoing project. An absolutely distortion-free Eucharist is not attainable within current parameters of human consciousness and performance.

(b) *All liturgy, and the Sunday Eucharist is particular, is negotiation.* The Sunday Eucharist is the complex of communicative acts in which the Christian community does not merely gather, nor merely become open to God's word and grace, nor merely worship, nor merely celebrate, nor merely express its faith, nor merely communicate among its members, but in which it negotiates. The people gathered in that assembly, and in a series of such assemblies, negotiate with one another about their common understanding of such important matters as the nature of the church, humanity, creation, and God. Within this negotiation the community receives, reinterprets, and passes on its mission, its history, and its scriptures. This negotiation is never a negotiation simply among equals, and hence the negotiation is also a negotiation about the power and service relationships among them, i.e., it is also a negotiation about how their church actually works.

(c) *Liturgy is not the only place in which such negotiation takes place.* It takes place also in meetings, in seminars, retreats, etc. and particularly in meetings for liturgical evaluation or planning. But liturgy, and Sunday Eucharist in particular, is the most important time and place of negotiation. Eucharist is the place in which this negotiation is placed in closest proximity to God and therefore achieves its strongest affirmation and authorization.

The way forward that is suggested here, then, is the way of negotiation which recognizes firstly that there is no perfect achievement of pure Eucharist but there is, rather, a constant uncovering of first one then another defect or distortion in current liturgical practice. Secondly, it recognizes that Eucharist is a primary place for negotiation with those *with whom* we currently disagree though within an overall common Christian identity. Those *with whom* we celebrate Eucharist include both those with whom we join in common consensus but also those with whom we disagree but desire to sort our way through those things most important to us.

What Are the Theological Principles at Issue Here?

(1) Does Eucharist always have the same value whenever and with whomsoever it is celebrated?

It is possible, and indeed common, to regard Eucharist as primarily a channel or occasion of divine grace. In such a view it is the essence or core action of Eucharist that is valuable. Attention, therefore, to the patterns of symbols which create such things as inclusive and exclusive language, leadership, relevant and irrelevant language, and the integration of historical and natural symbols, are peripheral to or even distractions from the act of divine love which is the essential core of Eucharist. In this view then, it is this essential core of Eucharist as channel or occasion of divine grace that is important regardless of whenever and with whomsoever Eucharist is celebrated.

Such an understanding of Eucharist does not need to, and indeed should not, be overly concerned with issues about with whom and how often Eucharist is celebrated. The divine action is here regarded either as independent of the eucharistic symbolism or as confined tightly and minimally within one or two special moments such as the proclaimed word, the consecration of the elements, or the invocation of the Spirit. The rest of the liturgy is window dressing to these central moments.

Attention to the whole complex of symbols which constitute a Eucharist, rather than to an abstract essence or special moments which embody that essence, requires a different view of the divine action in Eucharist. This second view emphasizes the divine action primarily as the assembly of believers gathered in the Eucharist. The divine action is here a varied and multiple one, for the assembly itself is constituted by a variety of participation, ministries, and leadership. There are here a great number of symbols or communicative acts by which this assembly is constituted precisely as an assembly of believers and not simply a juxtapositioning of individuals. In this view, then, all the communicative acts which occur within and constituting that assembly are "carriers," so to speak, of the one whole and complex divine action. Some symbols will be more important and more central than others. There will likely be high points and deep troughs. Some symbols may be trivial in isolation, but they are all elements which make up an important whole. They are not irrelevant.

This second view of Eucharist must include a concern for the combinations of symbols which contribute to such issues as leadership, inclusiveness, and relevancy because it is these combinations of symbols by which the divine action molds a people to be more godlike or by which these same people resist and divert the divine action. This view thus pays attention to the possibility that a particular Eucharist may not be beneficial but may rather be harmful to some or all of the participants. It must therefore also become concerned about with whom and how often Eucharist is celebrated, i.e., with the identity of the participants and the frequency of participation. It is this second view which gives rise to the issues addressed in this chapter.

(2) Symbolic distortion.

I have raised above the possibility that a Eucharist (i.e., a particular instance of Eucharist, not of course the idea of Eucharist in general) may be harmful rather than beneficial to some or all of the participants. We need to look more closely here at this possibility and I want to address it under the title of "symbolic distortion." Almost everyone agrees that liturgical performance at Eucharist is not always perfect. There are different points of view, however, on how, or with what seriousness, we are to treat these failures in performance.

These different points of view, simplified to the two most basic ones, arise according to whether we see the divine action in the Eucharist as occurring through one or two major symbols, or whether on the other hand, we see the divine action rather as the whole complex of symbols which constitute a particular Eucharist. The basic difference that concerns us here may be expressed as the difference between a "minimalist" view of liturgy and a "maximalist" view of liturgy.

A *minimalist* view looks at the minimum possible conditions for a valid Eucharist. If these conditions are present, then the Eucharist is valid and we can rely on the salvific presence of God among us. If these conditions are not present, then we are dealing with human actions for better or for worse, but in any case not "Eucharist." The traditional distinction earlier between the "sacrament" and "ecclesiastical rites" is consistent with this view. Within this view, the "sacrament" either occurs or it does not. Mistakes in this central sacramental action are serious since they may render the sacrament invalid. In any case the central action of the sacrament is either valid or invalid, and there is no point in talking about symbolic distortion. "Ecclesiastical rites," on the other hand, are essentially embellishments to that central action. They do not matter very much as far as God's salvific action is concerned. Mistakes are unfortunate and may be illicit, but the sacrament itself still occurs and that is the important thing. Thus in this view, mistakes in "ecclesiastical rites" do not warrant serious attention as "distortions" of the intended purposes of the Eucharist for the Eucharist occurs validly anyway in spite of such mistakes.

A *maximalist* view, on the other hand, is interested in the whole complex of symbols which occur within a Eucharist. It is the combination of these symbols in an instance of Eucharist that in greater or lesser degree affects the participants in benevolent or harmful ways and which constitutes the manifold divine action of Eucharist. This view requires an intense concern about the possibility that some symbols within that complex of symbols which constitute a Eucharist may have the effect of distorting the intended effect of that Eucharist. It is this view of Eucharist that gives rise to concern about with whom and how often we celebrate Eucharist. Thus, for example, consistently and seriously distorted instances of Eucharist raise questions about whether one should participate in them at all. Similarly, instances of Eucharist with dominating leadership patterns or containing discrimination against gender or culture raise concerns about whether we should avoid such Eucharists and participate in Eucharist only with those who are prepared to eliminate such symbolic distortions from their Eucharists.

(3) Eucharist as negotiation.

We are more accustomed to thinking of Eucharist in terms of such concepts as "channel of grace," "occasion for God's sovereign action," "self-communication of God," "word of God," "sacrament," "worship," "divine liturgy," "celebration," "mystery," than as *negotiation*. We cannot of course sum up the meaning of Eucharist in any one such concept and a certain multiplicity of terms is necessary. The concept of *negotiation* highlights some aspects of Eucharist (and of liturgy in general) that tend to be shadowed in most more traditional concepts.

One of the problems with a concept like negotiation is that it seems to take the divinity and the mystery out of liturgy and make it look too much like a very human and political marketplace. On the other hand though, such a concept does help us to avoid the opposite tendency where we over-spiritualize, or perhaps over-sanitize, our thinking about liturgy so that we are unable to recognize the serious human mistakes that can occur there and the power of our symbols for both good and harm.

I have outlined above something of what is implied in the notion of negotiation. These may be listed again more succinctly here:

(a) The correction of distortion in liturgy is an ongoing project of trying to get our symbols right so that they adequately communicate the divine. This corrective action is thus intrinsic to the action of liturgy and is a normal part of the responsibility of all participants especially where that liturgy is regular and frequent.

(b) In liturgy, and in Sunday Eucharists in particular as a series of regular assemblies, people influence one another's basic beliefs and understandings. In this interchange common understandings, priorities, and alliances are established or maintained.

(c) In such liturgical interchange, people continually reinterpret their own communal and individual identity in terms of their common mission, their history, and their scriptures.

(d) The power relationships within these liturgical assemblies are seldom equal and every liturgy is concerned with the maintenance or realignment of these relationships of power and service.

(e) Liturgy is not the only place in which such negotiation takes place. But in the Christian community, liturgy in general and Eucharist in particular are usually the most important places of negotiation because of their proximity to God. An understanding of Eucharist nevertheless needs to take into account the other negotiations which take place before, after, and between a series of Eucharists in the same community.

My purpose here is not to list every implication of the concept of negotiation when applied to Eucharist. The above list illustrates some of these implications—sufficient, I think, for our purposes here. The idea that Eucharist is a negotiation is an extension of the idea that Eucharist is "effective," i.e., the purpose of participating in Eucharist is that we be changed by it. But the life-giving and life-changing action of God in Eucharist is not something completely different from the communicative acts which constitute that Eucharist. The effectiveness of Eucharist lies within the communicative acts which constitute that Eucharist.

The concept of *negotiation* highlights the point that in Eucharist (a) the participants influence one another in complex and cumulative ways, and (b) they have a stake in the outcome—this is not an idle discussion nor mere play acting.

What Are the Practical Liturgical Effects?

Considerations of with whom and how often to celebrate Eucharist which focus on Eucharist as negotiation lead to the following major kinds of liturgical effects.

(1) One type of practical liturgical effect derives from the action of participants who come to recognise discriminatory symbols in the Eucharists in which they customarily participate and whose response to this recognition is *withdrawal*. There are a number of reasons why people might withdraw from their customary participation in a particular community's Eucharists. We are concerned here, however, only with the case where the reason for the withdrawal is precisely the recognition of defects in the symbolism. This strategy of withdrawal means that negotiation ceases. The defects in the symbolism of that Eucharist remain. The major liturgical effect is the cessation of participation by those persons, at least temporarily. Such a deliberate and informed withdrawal is based upon either a perception of Eucharist in terms of some model other than "negotiation" (e.g., Eucharist should be celebration or channel of grace or worship, but in fact in this case is not and therefore is in some sense false), or upon the decision that in this case there is little hope for a successful conclusion to this negotiation and it is not therefore worth the energy and effort. The liturgical effects here, then, are the withdrawal of some persons from those Eucharists and an absence of negotiation about those discriminatory symbols.

(2) A second response to the recognition of discriminatory symbols in Eucharist is the opposite of the above, namely, the *entry into negotiation* with the specific objective of replacing those discriminatory symbols with authentic ones. This strategy is based upon the perception both that Eucharist itself is in a fundamental way a negotiation among participants and that there is hope for a successful conclusion to these particular objectives in the negotiation. Some of the strategies of this negotiation have been described previously especially in the chapter on inclusive language. Note though that negotiation occurs both inside and outside Eucharist (especially in liturgical planning sessions), but the most important negotiations are those which occur within the eucharistic liturgy itself. The liturgical effects here are a deliberately engaged negotiation centered on the replacement of discriminatory symbols in those Eucharists.

(3) The two kinds of liturgical effects described above (withdrawal and negotiation) derive from the actions of *participants* who recognize discriminatory symbols in their customary Eucharists. These effects differ from each other in that one is the result of a decision for withdrawal from those Eucharists while the other is the result of a decision to enter into a specifically focused negotiation. A third kind of liturgical effect derives from the position adopted by those who are already the major *decision-makers* in a community's eucharistic liturgies. These are the people who have the most influence in the planning and performance of Eucharist. A way forward centered on the notion of Eucharist as negotiation has two main thrusts. On the one hand it presents these decision-makers with questions such as: Who are the people who no longer participate in our Eucharists, and is their withdrawal a legitimate protest against discriminatory symbols? Who are the people who have never been here but probably would be here if our symbols allowed them to be at home here? On the other hand, and with more immediacy, an understanding of Eucharist as negotiation makes current decision-makers aware of the existence and legitimacy of people already currently engaged in a negotiation to change discriminatory symbols. These people are not just conservers of the status quo, nor merely radical innovators for change's sake, but are participants and partners in the continuing negotiation which is at the heart of Christian Eucharist.

(4) There is at least one kind of liturgical effect we would hope to *avoid* here. This is the breaking up of local Eucharists into entirely interest-group or common-bond Eucharists, i.e., a situation where almost everyone opts for *minimal* negotiation. This effect occurs sometimes because participants in Eucharist misjudge the relative importance of discriminatory symbols or because their actions are, in fact, based on a strategy of moral purity rather than negotiation. Sometimes, however, a local community is content with or resists change of discriminatory symbols, and those opposed to such discrimination have no

alternative but to seek a more authentically Christian eucharistic liturgy elsewhere.

Beyond Liturgy

Defects in a community's symbolism contribute to or reinforce discriminations in the community's behavior and relationships outside liturgy as well those of society at large. One of the principal intentions of eliminating defects in the symbolism of Eucharist is to cease the contribution the Eucharist may be making, contrary to its intended purpose, to discrimination both within the Christian community and in society at large.

The more positive correlative effect is the contribution which Eucharist can make to achieving justice, i.e., in this case, a non-discriminatory society. The regular Eucharist of a Christian community constantly seeking God's justice in its most important expression of its own belief and identity contributes to the living out of this justice within the Christian community itself and to bringing it about in society at large.

Conclusion

In the previous chapters I have been concerned with five issues which arise from the gatherings of Christians in Eucharist. The attempt to deal with these liturgical issues has also required me to take a stand on some broader theological principles. I refer to these as "broader theological principles" because they are points at which liturgical symbolism overflows the strict confines of liturgical practice and affects other areas of practice and belief such as church organization, community identity, the force of tradition, images of God, catholicity, the relationship between church and society, the human relationship to Earth, as well as the nature of the Eucharist itself.

We may regard such theological principles as the *foundations* for our liturgical symbolism, or conversely we may regard them as the *implications* of our liturgical symbolism. In any case they are strands of the complex interchange between liturgy and the rest of Christian life. In respect to each liturgical issue I have tried to make explicit within its own chapter the main theological options that are commonly taken. I have also stated the theological option on which my own proposal for a way forward is based or to which it will lead us.

In addition to these broader theological principles which I have discussed *within* each chapter, there a some further principles which, rather than relating to particular issues and particular chapters, have guided this entire presentation. These principles are more specifically *liturgical* principles than are the broader theological principles referred to above. These liturgical principles concern (a) the relationship between liturgy and life, and (b) the nature of liturgical inculturation.

Liturgy and Life

The first of these liturgical principles has appeared here and there in the preceding chapters and is implicit in the structure of the presentation of each issue. This principle is that of *the mutual interchange between the Sunday Eucharist and the rest of Christian life*. The heading "Beyond Liturgy" within each chapter, although brief, summarizes in each case the purpose for engaging at all in an attempt to deal with the issue. The points made under this heading within each chapter are thus intended to indicate the way in which a change in eucharistic symbolism is likely to effect a change in the subsequent behavior and attitudes of the participants.

But the relationship between liturgical and non-liturgical behavior is not just a one way movement. It is a constant interchange. The issues that I have discussed in the previous chapters arose at least partly because of the influence, or because of the requirements, of non-liturgical aspects of Christian life. Issues of leadership, inclusive language, relevant language, our relationship to the natural cycles of Earth, and social discrimination become liturgical issues because they are already issues in society. They become central or urgent liturgical issues in one culture more than another, not because of the scriptural or historical foundations of liturgy, but because the social, political, and personal emphases of that culture have changed.

Let us refer to this interchange between the liturgical and the non-liturgical life of Christians more cryptically if less accurately as the interchange between liturgy and "life." I say "less accurately" because it seems to downplay the enormous formative, effective, and self-identifying influence of the ritual aspects of human life. It seems, in other words, to treat liturgy as if it were somehow not "life." On the assumption, however, that anyone who is concerned about the subject matter of this book is unlikely to make such a mistake, we may be content here with the simpler and more common expression "liturgy and life" where "life" is a shorthand for "non-liturgical life."

I have tried to intimate in the previous chapters that this interchange between liturgy and life is one of the major keys to liturgical planning and evaluation. I do not want to imply that there are not other things to do and other things in liturgy to talk about. But a focus on the interchange between liturgy and life tunes us into the central issues. It tunes us into the ways in which discriminations and non-Christian practices have crept into, or are being resisted by, our liturgical symbols. And it tunes us into the ways in which our liturgical symbols can deal with, or are impotent toward, such practices in our society.

I have also wanted to emphasize that this interchange is continuous. There is no point in Christian history when we can hope to say that our liturgies have now reached a satisfactory state requiring no more change nor reformation. Recent liturgical reform has been resourced and critiqued by studies of scripture and liturgical history. But the driving force for those reforms is the contemporary interchange between liturgy and life. This driving force can be guided by historical solutions and historical precedents but it is not put to rest by them. Even the attempt to disengage liturgy from changes in society is itself a particular kind of response, a protective response, to the interchange between liturgy and life. The exercise that I have attempted in the previous chapters accepts the continuous nature of liturgical reform. It attempts to focus on central issues within that interchange which require attention at this particular time, though they may not always have required attention. We can hope that they may no longer require attention in the future. But in that case they will be replaced by other issues requiring our attention.

On the more positive side, a focus on the interchange between liturgy and life helps us to articulate particular strands of God's graciousness in the whole of our lives, that is, in both the liturgical and the non-liturgical parts of our lives. Liturgy, in other words, is not just an articulation of God's graciousness, it is also an indication of where that graciousness may be found in the rest of our lives. More particularly, a focus on the interchange between liturgy and life opens us to be receptive to that graciousness, explicitly even if not always accurately proclaimed in liturgy, which pervades the whole of our lives but to which some parts of our lives have previously been closed.

Liturgical Inculturation

The second of the liturgical principles which has guided the previous chapters and which needs some explanation here is that of *the process of liturgical inculturation.*

First, it is specifically the nature of *liturgical* inculturation that concerns us here rather than inculturation in the more general sense which needs to be concerned with a broader spectrum of matters, such as the inculturation of church organization, the inculturation of belief and doctrine, the inculturation of pastoral care, the translation of biblical texts. Second, we can make yet a further refinement and note that it is not liturgical inculturation as a whole that concerns us here, but the again more confined matter of the liturgical inculturation of *standard* rites.

By using the term "standard rites" I mean to indicate that we are dealing here not with newly created rites but with rites which already exist and which already have a name and an expected pattern of symbols. The Eucharist is this kind of rite. The process of inculturation which concerns us here begins, then, not from nothing, nor from some general principles or beliefs about what *should* happen, but with a standard rite which already exists and has been "handed on" to us. It already exists, not just in the sense that someone has told us about its existence somewhere else, nor just in the sense that we have read a book about how to do it, but in the sense that we already participate in it though we did not create it ourselves.

In this case then, the need for inculturation arises because these standard rites are perceived to be in some ways inadequate. Commonly this has occurred because the rites have travelled from one culture to another, or from one generation to another. The originating culture or generation "hands on" what it can, namely a rite which to the best of their ability is both faithful to its Christian foundations and has been modified to communicate well within that originating culture or generation. The recipient culture or generation begins with what it has received and to the best of its ability modifies that received rite so that it is again both faithful to its Christian foundation and communicates well within the recipient culture or generation.

I have used the term "handed on" to indicate that standard rites are *traditional*. Not all rites are traditional. Some have been recently created by a community for their own particular and regular use. Others may be created simply for one particular occasion without any intention to repeat them. Eucharist, however, falls into the category of a traditional rite. In that sense it has been "handed on." But we should perhaps be cautious about our metaphors here. These metaphors can be helpful, but can sometimes be misleading. As a metaphor within considerations of inculturation, the "handing on" metaphor can be misleading because it can be taken to imply that traditional rites like Eucharist are something which we acquire, possess, and then convey to others. But there is too much implication of human control here and we may need to take note that rites are not handed on in the sense that a belief, or a custom, or a "deposit of faith," for example, can be acquired by people and then conveyed to others.

Traditional rites control people more than people control rites. We participate in them rather than assimilate or possess them. If we are to use body metaphors we would be better to draw upon the action of breathing rather than the action of hands as our metaphor for the relation between people and traditional rites. Traditional rites breathe people in, in the sense that people are drawn inside, to become participants. Once inside, the participants enliven the rites and can modify those rites, but they cannot radically change them without danger to the whole body except over quite long periods of time. The participants are then breathed out again, for people do not stay within a rite for long, but the people themselves have been modified by the process of inhalation and exhalation. The people come and go, but the rites remain, though both people and rites are mutually modified one by the other.

Another metaphor that deserves consideration here is one which illustrates liturgical inculturation as burning a candle at both ends so that eventually the flames meet in the middle. The ends in this case are on the one hand the cultural patterns of a people, and on the other hand the authorized texts which control the performance of a standard rite. This metaphor implies that liturgical inculturation begins with two distinct elements each identifiable in its own right: cultural patterns on the one hand, and authorized texts on the other. The process of liturgical inculturation then consists in bringing together these two elements to form a new dynamic whole.[1] I mention this metaphor here because it represents a process of liturgical inculturation which is alternative to the one I have used in the previous chapters.

The process of inculturation which has engaged me in the previous chapters has not been one in which culture and liturgy have been brought together. It is not one in which standard rites have required translation into a new cultural pattern. Nor is it one in which a cultural dimension and a theological dimension have to be brought together. Rather, it has assumed that the standard rite, the Eucharist in this case, is already part of the cultural patterns of a people. But neither the culture, nor the standard rite within it, are entirely integrated and harmonious. In most contemporary cultures there are pluralist, borrowed, conflictual, and disjointed elements within them. The culture is no less "theological" than the liturgy, nor is the liturgy any less

---

[1] The metaphor is used most notably by Anscar Chupungco (*Liturgical Inculturation: Sacramentals, Religiosity, and Catechesis*, Collegeville, Minnesota: The Liturgical Press, 1992, especially pp. 32, 37–38, 64, 121). See also his *Liturgies of the Future: The Process and Methods of Inculturation*, New York/Mahwah: Paulist Press, 1989.

"cultural" than most of the other elements which make up the cultural patterns of a people.

Thus the process of liturgical inculturation which has engaged me in the previous chapters has been one which begins from participation in a liturgical rite. It assumes that this standard rite, whatever its origin, is currently an aspect or item in the cultural pattern of those participants. It does not assume, in other words, a traditional missionary situation where missionaries bring with them a standard rite which needs adaptation to a non-Christian culture. It assumes, rather, that the participants, i.e., those most concerned with effecting the liturgical inculturation, are quite at home within the cultural patterns of the place including the standard rite which they also regard as their own. Some of their current cultural patterns, including their liturgies, originated overseas. Their culture includes recently introduced foreign elements as well as recently created local elements. The standard rite, in other words, is part of their current cultural patterns, but like many other aspects of contemporary cultural patterns, the standard rite is also to some degree at odds with some other cultural patterns.

What initiates the process of inculturation in this case is not the need to bring two elements together (cultural patterns on the one hand and authorized texts on the other) but a perception of issues, of inadequacies, of some non-communicating symbols, or the potential for more communicative symbols within the current performance of the rite. Liturgical inculturation begins, then, with some dissatisfaction within the liturgical performance itself. Only later do authorized texts begin to be examined. And they are then examined both for what they may provide in terms of a solution as also with an awareness that they may themselves be a cause of the dissatisfaction.

By way of summary, then, I have based the previous chapters on an understanding of the *liturgical* inculturation of *standard* rites which entails the following points:

(1) Inculturation is a *process*.
In the liturgical inculturation of standard rites the process is

one in which a standard rite is gradually modified by the customs and sensitivities of a local culture. In liturgical matters there are sometimes attempts to propose new blueprints or new designs which need only implementation. A process, on the other hand, implies that there no single overall proposal but a continuing spiral of proposal and reproposal for the modification of the rites. Above all it is an ecclesial activity, that is, an activity in which a wide variety of church members participate.

Liturgies are not books, nor are they *in* books. They are not even in liturgical books. They are complex acts of face-to-face communication. Liturgical inculturation, therefore, does not take place in books. Books can, however, play a part in the process. The process that I have adopted in the previous chapters is to start always with issues which arise in actual liturgical performance. But the proposals for ways forward are themselves made here within a book with the intention of influencing future liturgical performance.

(2) The agents of liturgical inculturation are liturgical *participants*.

Liturgical inculturation may be planned by other people. It may be critiqued by other people. It may seek approval from other people. But it occurs only when enacted by liturgical participants.

Since liturgical inculturation is intimately about culture, it can be enacted only by persons who are intimately persons of that culture. It cannot be enacted by expatriate missionaries nor wellwishers from other cultures nor liturgical experts from other cultures. Liturgies eventually escape from the hands of those who brought them and speak directly to those who celebrate them.[2] Not all discussions of liturgical inculturation take sufficient heed of the difference between inculturation carried out by insiders and that carried out by outsiders to the culture con-

---

[2] This point is made by Richard Gray (*Black Christians and White Missionaries*, New Haven & London: Yale University Press, 1990, p. 1) and becomes a central theme in his book.

cerned. The difference is worth stressing here because two quite different processes are involved. I have been concerned in the previous chapters with inculturation carried out by insiders, those at home both in the culture and in the eucharistic liturgy which they celebrate. But, and this is very important, such inculturation can be encouraged, critiqued, and emulated by people from other cultures.

The process of liturgical inculturation occurs, then, when those people who are most familiar with those liturgies

(a) take seriously their own insights, and
(b) begin to discuss these in a serious and systematic way, with a view to
(c) evaluating, and then
(d) changing those liturgies
(e) grounded in a sense of responsibility to both the local and the universal church.

(3) Liturgical inculturation normally takes place as a series of *changes of bits and pieces*.

A liturgy is a complex act of face-to-face communication, and needs to be regarded as an integrated whole. But precisely because a liturgy itself is a complex but integrated whole, liturgical inculturation does not need to be done as a whole. That is to say, liturgical inculturation does not need to be envisaged in a holistic way as an interaction between a set of cultural patterns and a standard liturgical rite. Such an overall view is characteristic of outside observers, not of liturgical participants. We do need to see particular liturgies as integrated wholes where any modification of one part affects the overall integrity of symbols and meaning. But precisely because the integrity of symbols and meaning is a characteristic of the liturgies themselves, the process of inculturation can be carried out in bits and pieces.[3]

---

[3] Robert Taft (*Beyond East and West: Problems in Liturgical Understanding*, Washington, DC: Pastoral Press, 1984, p. 154) makes the conclusion from his researches in liturgical history that liturgies do not grow evenly like living organisms. Rather, their individual elements possess a life of their own.

The "bits and pieces" which have concerned me in the previous chapters have been particular issues which have arisen within the liturgical performance of Eucharists. The focus of concern has been the integrity of the eucharistic liturgies. But the process of inculturation represented in each of these chapters has focused on one issue at a time rather than on a wholesale rethinking of Eucharist within my own culture.

The process of inculturation may thus be represented as a movement from *attention* to *discernment* to *readjustment* which then calls for a new focus of *attention*. That is to say, liturgical inculturation is best regarded as a series of small decisions moving in a spiral of attention-discernment-readjustment-attention to particular sets of liturgical symbols. Our *attention* is drawn to a particular symbol or set of symbols because of a sense of non-fit or creative possibility. Any change to those symbols requires *discernment* of the cultural and theological appropriateness of possible new symbols. This may lead to a *readjustment* of current liturgical symbols. And this readjustment is likely in turn to bring other symbols to our attention.

Not all symbols require attention. Some sets of symbols are better simply left alone. Nor should we make the assumption that communication is increased by the adoption of familiar cultural symbols into liturgy. Communication can be increased as much by difference as by sameness. Nor again should we make the assumption that cultures are isolated. Most cultures are exposed to other cultures through migration and travel, as well as through films and television. We are constantly learning and adopting new styles of communication as well as constantly discarding familiar ones.

Only at a very abstract level can liturgical inculturation be regarded as a question of the essentials of the gospel message being brought into interaction with the characteristic traits of a particular culture. Liturgical inculturation when carried out by liturgical participants within a culture, rather than by missionaries or by a centralized authority in control of liturgical texts, operates by the continual decisions about particular liturgical-cultural issues.

Select Bibliography

Alexander, J. Neil. *Time and Community*. In honor of Thomas Julian Talley. Washington, DC: The Pastoral Press, 1990.

Baldovin, John F. *Worship: City, Church and Renewal*. Washington, DC: The Pastoral Press, 1991.

Bell, Catherine. *Ritual Theory, Ritual Practice*. New York: Oxford University Press, 1992.

Botte, Bernard. *From Silence to Participation: An Insider's View of Liturgical Renewal*. Washington, DC: The Pastoral Press, 1988.

Bugnini, Annibale. *The Reform of the Liturgy 1948–1975*. Collegeville, Minnesota: The Liturgical Press, 1990.

Cannadine, David, and Simon Price (eds.). *Rituals of Royalty: Power and Ceremonial in Traditional Societies*. Cambridge: Cambridge University Press, 1987.

Chupungco, Anscar. *Liturgical Inculturation: Sacramentals, Religiosity, and Catechesis*. Collegeville, Minnesota: The Liturgical Press, 1992.

————. *Liturgies of the Future: The Process and Methods of Inculturation*. New York/Mahwah: Paulist Press, 1989.

————. *Shaping the Easter Feast*. Washington, DC: The Pastoral Press, 1992.

Collins, Mary. *Worship: Renewal to Practice*. Washington, DC: The Pastoral Press, 1987.

Collins, Patrick W. *Bodying Forth: Aesthetic Liturgy*. New York/ Mahwah: Paulist Press, 1992.

Cooke, Bernard. *The Distancing of God: The Ambiguity of Symbol in History and Theology*. Minneapolis: Fortress Press, 1990.

Crockett, William R. *Eucharist: Symbol of Transformation*. New York: Pueblo, 1989.

Dillistone, F.W. *The Power of Symbols in Religion and Culture*. New York: Crossroad, 1986.

Driver, Tom F. *The Magic of Ritual: Our Need for Liberating Rites That Transform Our Lives and Our Communities*. San Francisco: HarperSanFrancisco, 1991.

Empereur, James L., and Christopher G. Kiesling. *The Liturgy That Does Justice*. Collegeville, Minnesota: The Liturgical Press, 1990.

Fink, Peter E. *Worship: Praying the Sacraments*. Washington, DC: The Pastoral Press, 1991.

Finn, Peter C., and James M. Schellman (eds.). *Shaping English Liturgy: Studies in Honor of Archbishop Denis Hurley*. Washington, DC: The Pastoral Press, 1990.

Francis, Mark R. *Liturgy in a Multicultural Community*. Collegeville, Minnesota: The Liturgical Press, 1991

Gitari, David (ed.). *Anglican Liturgical Inculturation in Africa*. Bramcote, Nottingham: Grove Books, 1994.

Grimes, Ronald L. *Ritual Criticism: Case Studies in Its Practice, Essays in Its Theory*. Columbia, South Carolina: University of South Carolina Press, 1990.

Gusmer, Charles. *Wholesome Worship*. Washington, DC: The Pastoral Press, 1989.

Harris, Chris. *Creating Relevant Rituals: Celebrations for Religious Education*. Newtown, Australia: EJ Dwyer, 1992.

Henderson, Frank, Stephen Larson, and Kathleen Quinn. *Liturgy, Justice and the Reign of God: Integrating Vision and Practice*. New York/Mahwah: Paulist Press, 1989.

Holeton, David R. (ed.). *Revising the Eucharist: Groundwork for the Anglican Communion*. Bramcote, Nottingham: Grove Books, 1994.

Kertzer, David I. *Ritual, Politics, and Power*. New Haven & London: Yale University Press, 1988.

Kilmartin, Edward J. *Christian Liturgy: Theology and Practice. I: Systematic Theology of Liturgy*. Kansas City: Sheed & Ward, 1988.

Lee, Bernard J. *The Eucharist*. Vol. 3 of Alternative Futures for Worship series. Collegeville, Minnesota: The Liturgical Press, 1987.

Madden, Lawrence J. (ed.). *The Awakening Church: 25 Years of Liturgical Renewal*. Collegeville, Minnesota: The Liturgical Press, 1992.

McCarthy, S. *Creation Liturgy: An Earth-centered Theology of Liturgy*. San Jose, California: Resource, 1987.

Minamiki, George. *The Chinese Rites Controversy from Its Beginning to Modern Times*. Chicago: Loyola University Press, 1985.

Power, David N. *Worship: Culture and Theology*. Washington, DC: The Pastoral Press, 1990.

Price, S.R.F. *Rituals and Power: The Roman Imperial Cult in Asia Minor*. Cambridge: Cambridge University Press, 1984.

Ramshaw-Schmidt, Gail. *Christ in Sacred Speech: The Meaning of Liturgical Language*. Philadelphia: Fortress Press, 1986.

Schmemann, Alexander. *The Eucharist: Sacrament of the Kingdom*. New York: St. Vladimir's Seminary Press, 1988.

Senn, Frank C. *The Witness of the Worshiping Community: Liturgy and the Practice of Evangelism*. New York/Mahwah: Paulist Press, 1993.

Stevenson, Kenneth W. *Accept This Offering: The Eucharist as Sacrifice Today*. Collegeville, Minnesota: The Liturgical Press, 1989.

———. *The First Rites: Worship in the Early Church*. Collegeville, Minnesota: The Liturgical Press, 1989.

Taft, Robert. *Beyond East and West: Problems in Liturgical Understanding*. Washington, DC: The Pastoral Press, 1984.

Talley, Thomas. *The Origins of the Liturgical Year*. New York: Pueblo, 1986.

———. *Worship: Reforming Tradition*. Washington, DC: The Pastoral Press, 1990.

Vogel, Cyrille. *Medieval Liturgy: An Introduction to the Sources*. Revised and translated by William G. Storey and Niels Krogh Rasmussen. Washington, DC: The Pastoral Press, 1986.

Wechsler, Howard J. *Offerings of Jade and Silk: Ritual and Symbol in the Legitimation of the T'ang Dynasty*. New Haven & London: Yale University Press, 1985.

Whalen, Michael D. *Seasons and Feasts of the Church Year: An Introduction*. New York/Mahwah: Paulist Press, 1993.

White, Susan J. *Christian Worship and Technological Change*. Nashville: Abingdon Press, 1994.

Wilde, James A. (ed.). *At That Time: Cycles and Seasons in the Life of a Christian*. Chicago: Liturgy Training Publications, 1989.

Winter, Miriam Therese. *WomanPrayer, WomanSong: Resources for Ritual*. Illustrated by Meinread Craighead. Oak Park, Illinois: Meyer-Stone, 1987.

Wren, Brian. *What Language Shall I Borrow: God-talk in Worship: A Male Response to Feminist Theology*. New York: Crossroad, 1989.

Yeow Choo Lak and John C. England (eds.). *Doing Theology with People's Symbols and Images*. ATESEA Occasional Papers: No. 8. Singapore: The Association for Theological Education in South East Asia, 1989.